Scoring with Logic® Pro

Jay Asher

Course Technology PTR
A part of Cengage Learning

COURSE TECHNOLOGY
CENGAGE Learning·

Australia • Brazil • Japan • Korea • Mexico • Singapore • Spain • United Kingdom • United States

COURSE TECHNOLOGY
CENGAGE Learning·

Scoring with Logic® Pro
Jay Asher

Publisher and General Manager,
Course Technology PTR: Stacy L. Hiquet

Associate Director of Marketing:
Sarah Panella

Manager of Editorial Services:
Heather Talbot

Senior Marketing Manager:
Mark Hughes

Acquisitions Editor: Orren Merton

Project Editor: Kim Benbow

Technical Reviewer: Peter Schwartz

Copy Editor: Tonya Cupp

Interior Layout Tech: MPS Limited

Cover Designer: Luke Fletcher

Indexer: BIM Indexing Services

Proofreader: Andy Saff

For product information and technology assistance, contact us at
Cengage Learning Customer & Sales Support, 1-800-354-9706
For permission to use material from this text or product,
submit all requests online at **www.cengage.com/permissions**
Further permissions questions can be emailed to
permissionrequest@cengage.com

Logic Pro, Mac, and Mac OS are trademarks of Apple Inc., registered in the U.S. and other countries.

All other trademarks are the property of their respective owners.

All images © Cengage Learning unless otherwise noted.

Library of Congress Control Number: 2012930791

ISBN-13: 978-1-133-69334-5

ISBN-10: 1-133-69334-2

Course Technology, a part of Cengage Learning
20 Channel Center Street
Boston, MA 02210
USA

Cengage Learning is a leading provider of customized learning solutions with office locations around the globe, including Singapore, the United Kingdom, Australia, Mexico, Brazil, and Japan. Locate your local office at: **international.cengage.com/region**

Cengage Learning products are represented in Canada by Nelson Education, Ltd.

For your lifelong learning solutions, visit **courseptr.com**

Visit our corporate website at **cengage.com**

Printed in the United States of America
1 2 3 4 5 6 7 14 13 12

This book is dedicated to my family and friends who have supported and encouraged me throughout my life and career: my lovely, smart, and talented daughter, Emily Marissa; my parents, Sherman and Renee Altshuler; my late grandparents, who I feel are always with me; my aunts and uncles; Jon Feltheimer, who believed in my talent early on and has always been there for me; and my fellow composers and musicians, whose brilliance, creativity, and commitment are a constant inspiration.

Especially, this book is dedicated to my lovely wife, partner, best friend, teacher, soulmate, and self-described computer widow, Rosemary, whose belief in me is my daily sustenance.

Acknowledgments

There are so many people I would like to thank, and I know I am going to miss a few, so please let me apologize in advance if I have omitted mentioning you.

First of all, I would like to thank my friend Orren Merton, who shocked me by offering me the opportunity to write this book; my stalwart tech editor, Peter Schwartz, for keeping me honest and catching things that I flat out missed or got wrong; and my conscientious editor, Kim Benbow, for her attention to detail.

Finally, I would like to thank my EmApple friends, some of whom I have known since I first started using C-Lab Notator on the Atari, back when dinosaurs still roamed the earth, and some of whom I have met more recently: Bob Hunt, Gerhard Lengeling, Chris Adam, Clemens Homburg, Manfred Knauff, Thorsten Adam, and Robert Brock.

About the Author

Jay Asher is a composer, songwriter, arranger, orchestrator, conductor, pianist/synthesist, and entertainer who has been based in Los Angeles since 1972.

He was raised in the Boston area and is a graduate of the Boston Conservatory of Music with a B.M. in music composition. He did post-graduate orchestration study with renowned Los Angeles orchestrator Dr. Albert Harris.

As a composer, he has written music scores and songs for many TV series, TV Movies of the Week, and films, most notably New World Television's *Zorro*. He has written songs that have been recorded by Julio Iglesias, Whitney Houston, and Donna Summer, among others. He has also produced and arranged CDs for the Israeli-based duo Merkava. Among the films and TV movies he has arranged, orchestrated and/or conducted for are Paramount Pictures' *Blame It On Rio* and NBC's TV mini-series *JFK: Reckless Youth*.

He has served as a musical director and/or accompanist for such artists as Neil Diamond, Bobby Gentry, Carol Burnett, Minnie Riperton, Donald O' Connor, and Roslyn Kind, as well as playing piano/keyboards for various TV and film projects and commercials. He has also been featured as the lead vocalist on songs for several TV movies and films, including Disney's *Under Wraps*.

A monthly contributor to *Film Music Magazine* and MacPro Video's The Hub, Jay is also a Level 2 Apple Certified Trainer for Logic Pro 9 and the author of *Going Pro with Logic Pro 9* (2010) and *Going Pro with Logic Pro 8* (2008), both by Course Technology PTR.

Contents

Introduction

Thank you for your interest in this book. Back in the early 1990s, I was hired to compose the music for a new TV series, *Zorro*. I needed an application that could do MIDI sequencing *and* score printout. The clear choice was C Lab's Notator for the Atari platform. After that platform died, the geniuses behind C Lab became Emagic, and Notator morphed into the Macintosh-based program, Logic. The Score Editor morphed with it, and it continued to be my choice for MIDI sequencing and score printout.

Over the years, Logic became cross-platform, added audio capabilities, became Macintosh again when Apple purchased Emagic, and we are now at Logic Pro 9. What is surprising (and disappointing) to some is how little real change has occurred in the Score Editor. As a result, Johannes Prischl's excellent book, *The Logic Notation Guide*, is still the bible.

What *has* changed for many users since Prischl's book was written is the terminology and how we work. Many of us now use a lot of software instruments rather than hardware MIDI, and we address these in Logic directly rather than using Logic's MIDI and multi-instruments. Many others use a combination of both.

The Prischl book was intended to teach users everything there is to know about using Logic's Score Editor, from player-ready parts to engraved quality scores. However, today engraved scores are more likely to be done in applications designed primarily for score work, like Finale or Sibelius. Logic is more likely to be used for printing out parts and scores for recording sessions, rehearsals, and so on, with projects that were composed in Logic, and it is obviously an advantage to be able to stay in one application for the whole job.

So why this book? Many would-be Logic score users have joined the ranks in recent years and there is no book that uses the current terminology nor has screenshots of Logic Pro 9. This book will focus on a practical approach to preparing parts and scores for recording sessions and rehearsals. It is geared toward Logic Pro users who have a solid grip on the basics of using the application and a knowledge of sequencing, but who have not yet invested the time in learning to use the Score Editor fully.

The book consists of 22 tutorials. My criteria for choosing topics was determined by my own use and how often I have been asked by others on the best way to do so. I apologize if I did not get to your favorites.

Have fun!

1 Strategies for Preparing Parts and Scores in Logic Pro 9

I ts environment is what separates Logic Pro from the pack. Using some rather complex tricks with meta events, transformers, and the like, you can make a project sound just as you wish and print the parts and a conductor's score all in the same project.

I do not work this way, as I believe it involves making choices that I simply do not wish to make. Typically, I first complete a version of the project that sounds exactly the way I want it to sound, and includes material that will augment the real players. Then I do two more versions: one for a full score and one for the parts.

Consolidating Regions for Length of Project Tracks

Now you can start transforming your "sound perfect" project into a printable score. Open M27 (which clearly does not sound perfect) and save it as M27 Full Score. From now on, you no longer care what this project sounds like, but only what it looks like.

Assume that all 12 instruments here contain parts that are to be performed by real players. To make these parts readable for players, the parts should conform to the project length so that every measure in every part will be visible, in this case, 24 measures. Consolidate regions so there is one length of project region per track.

The first obstacle is individual regions potentially not being quantized or having different settings. Because MIDI position affects the display, you should perhaps quantize all the regions destructively. Remember, this is a copy and you need not worry how it sounds.

Track 10 is a piano track with two regions. Both are quantized to 8th notes in the Extended Region Parameters Box in the Inspector; the first is set to a Q-Strength of 90%, while the second region is set to 83%. Because they are set to different Q-Strengths, in the Inspector you see a + when both regions are selected, as in Figure 1.1.

1. Reset all the regions to a Q-Strength of 100%.

2. Click on the Piano track in the Track List and notice that both regions are selected.

3. Since both regions have the same quantization, you can merge them in the Arrange Window's local Region menu > Merge > Regions, as you can see in Figure 1.2. The better

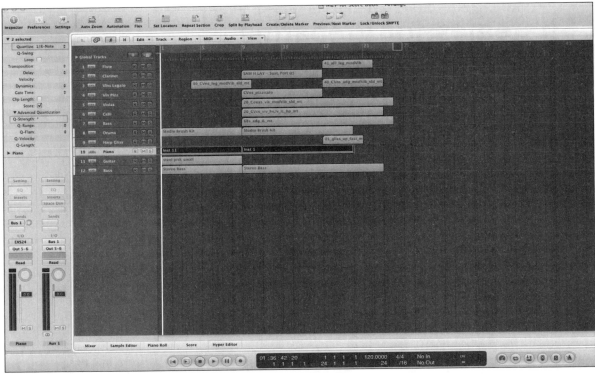

Figure 1.1 A region is set to a Q-Strength of 90% as seen in the Extended Region Parameters Box in the Inspector.

Figure 1.2 Merge regions.

way is, as always, by a key command. LP9 defaults to the equal sign just to the left of the right delete key as a shortcut.

But what if the first region was quantized to a 16th note and the second was quantized to an 8th note? In this case, you would need to perform another step before merging them.

4.   With the regions selected, go to the Arrange Window's local MIDI menu. Choose Region Parameters > Apply Quantization Settings Destructively (Q). See Figure 1.3.

5.   Merge the regions on Track 8 and Track 10. The Arrange Window should look like what you see in Figure 1.4.

Figure 1.3 Apply quantization settings destructively.

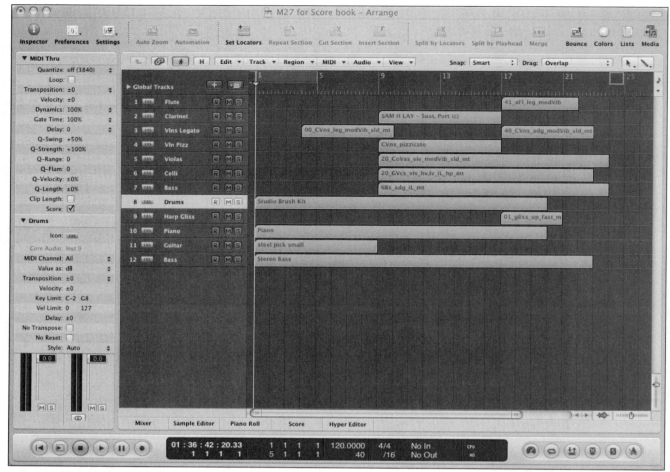

Figure 1.4 Tracks 8 and 10 have merged regions.

The next issue we have to confront is that most of the tracks do not have a region at the beginning of the project nor do they end at the end of the project. Although there are other methods (like dragging the lower-left corner of the regions to 1 1 1 1), I prefer to use the Pencil tool.

This is one of many instances where key commands are your friend. There are key commands for Set Region/Event/Marquee Start to Playhead Position and Set Region/Event/Marquee End to Playhead Position. See Figure 1.5.

6. Select all the regions by hitting Command-A and then navigate to the beginning of the project, 1 1 1 1.

7. Press the key command combo to perform Set Region/Event/Marquee Start to Playhead Position. Notice that all the regions now begin at the beginning of the project in Figure 1.6.

Figure 1.5 The key commands for setting the region's beginning and end in the Key Commands Window.

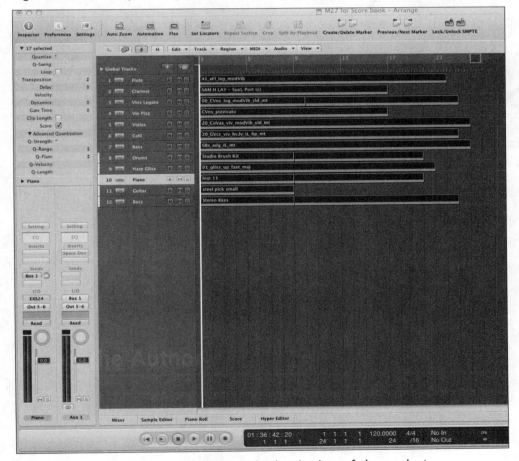

Figure 1.6 All regions now begin at the beginning of the project.

8. Set the playhead to the end of the project.

9. Press the key command combo to perform Set Region/Event/Marquee End to Playhead
    Position. Your Arrange Window should now look like Figure 1.7.

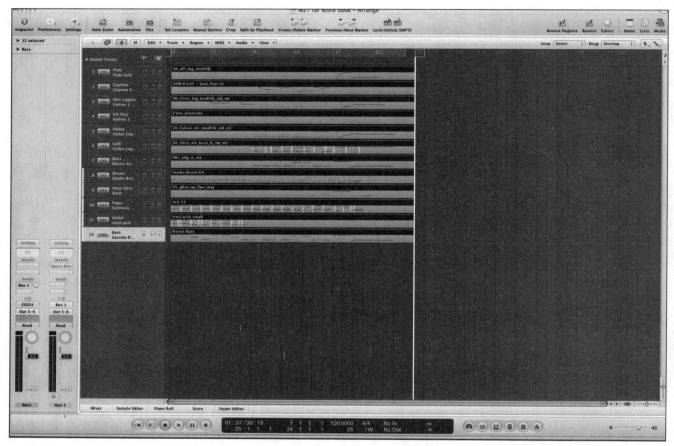

Figure 1.7 The Arrange Window with all regions extended to the end of the project.

2 Getting to Know the Score Editor

You will want to be comfortable with some elements of the Score Editor when you are working in it.

Viewing in the Score Editor with Links

Starting with Logic Pro 8, Apple introduced the all-in-one Arrange Window. The Score Editor is available either by clicking the Score tab or typing N on your keyboard. Many people love being able to access so many editors in one window—especially those with limited screen real estate (like laptop users) and people who came from applications like Digital Performer (which does most things in one window). Personally, I would rather have bamboo inserted under my finger nails than try to do anything but the most rudimentary score prep in that Score Editor window. I recommend creating a screenset with a Score Window, as I did with Screenset 2. (I assume you know how to do this. If you do not, search for "screenset" in the LP9 manual.)

Note When you are working in the Score Editor, size *does* matter. I have two monitors, and generally my Score Editor takes up the entire second monitor for this kind of work.

Even many long-time Logic users do not have a handle on how the different links work. Starting with LP8, this lack of knowledge was complicated by the fact that the Piano Roll editor works differently than the Score Editor. It is important to get a good handle on the link behavior.

1. Open Screenset 2. You will see a Score Editor with a minimized Arrange Window. The Score Editor has the Show Content link (yellow) engaged with the default score set (more on these later) called All Instruments. See Figure 2.1.

2. Scroll down through the track list. The Score Editor updates to show you the contents of each region as it is selected.

3. Click the Link button in the Score Editor until it turns violet, which indicates a Same Level link, and now you see all the regions. If you highlight the Oboe and Clarinet regions, they become highlighted in the Score Editor as well. See Figure 2.2.

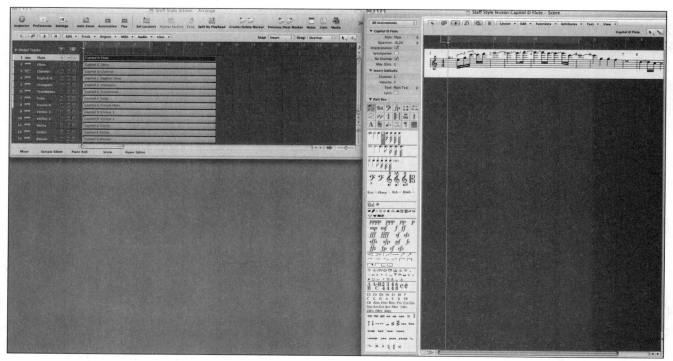

Figure 2.1 A screenset with a minimized Arrange Window and the Score Editor with the Show Content link.

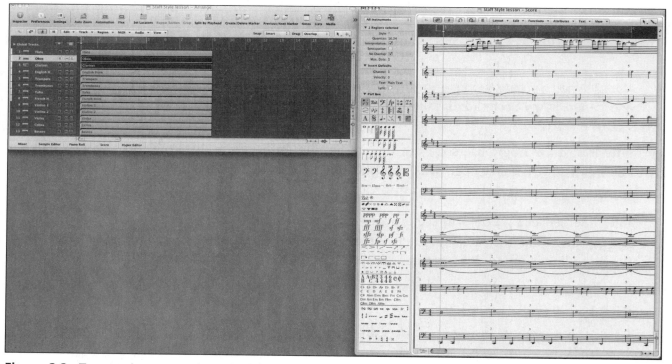

Figure 2.2 Two regions are selected with the Same Level link engaged in the Score Editor.

4. Return to the Content link in the Score Editor and highlight the Flute region. The score display will update.

5. Click the link in the Score Editor to display a gray icon (No Link mode). Select a different region. The Score Editor does not update, but keeps showing the contents of the Flute region.

Buttons, Menus, and the Inspector in the Score Editor

As with all Logic Pro windows, the Score Editor has buttons and menus running across the top. See Figure 2.3.

Figure 2.3 Buttons and menus in the Score Editor.

The first button, Hierarchy, changes the view to show all the regions in the score set, even though the Show Content link is still engaged. You can return to the previous view by double-clicking any region in the Score Editor. If you have locked the screenset (and I always do), you can instead simply type the key number (2 in this case). Then you see the Link and the Catch, as well as the MIDI In and MIDI Out buttons. As I said in the introduction, this book assumes you are pretty familiar with Logic Pro so I will not provide an explanation of the latter three. If you are not familiar with them, spend a little time with the manual.

The next button after the MIDI Out button is unique to the Score Editor. It toggles between the default Linear View and Page View, as reflected in Figure 2.4. Generally, you want to insert

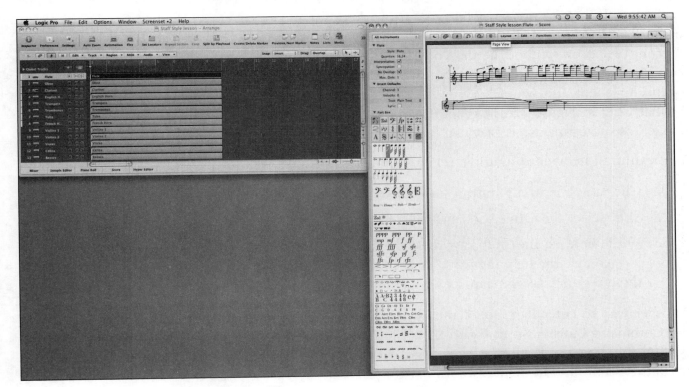

Figure 2.4 The Score Editor with Page View.

symbols, text, lyrics, and so on while you are working in Linear View. Switch to Page View when you are formatting your parts and scores for printout.

A quick perusal of the Layout, Edit, Functions, Attributes, Text, and View menus gives you an idea of just how serious Logic Pro's Score Editor is and how much control you can have, given familiarity and elbow grease. More on these menus later.

As you can with the Arrange Window, you can show or hide the Inspector by typing I. The Inspector shows some similar elements to what you see in the Arrange Window but with some very significant differences (see Figure 2.5). From top to bottom in the Inspector you see the following:

- Score Set choice.
- Display Parameter Box, whose settings apply to the selected regions.
- Event Parameter Box, which applies to any selected events.
- Part Box, which has sets of types of notes, rests, symbols, trills, crescendos and diminuendos, and so on.
- A symbol palette, which changes as you choose a different group in the Part Box.

Entering Items from the Part Box into Regions in the Score Editor

In typical Logic Pro fashion, there are a number of ways to enter items from the Part Box into regions in the Score Editor. The most obvious way is to simply drag items from the palette into the region. If you do not see what you are looking for in the palette, click the appropriate group in the Part Box; you will then see it. Keep an eye on the yellow help tag to make sure you are inserting items or symbols at the correct bar/beat position. In Figure 2.6, you will see a mezzo forte symbol and a crescendo symbol that I simply dragged in. I can make the crescendo symbol extend its length and width by grabbing the upper-right handle and dragging it out and up. That is what I did in Figure 2.7. In general, however, I advise waiting until you switch to Page View to make those adjustments, as they can look quite different there, depending on the formatting you do.

You can drag items into multiple regions simultaneously as well.

1. Click the Hierarchy button (arrow) so you can see all the regions.
2. Shift-select the Oboe, Clarinet, and English horn regions.
3. While holding the Shift key, drag the MF (mF or mf) symbol into the Oboe region. Notice that the help tag says "Insert Multi." Now you have inserted the mf symbol on all three regions, as you can see in Figure 2.8.

Another way to enter Part Box symbols is with the Pencil tool. By default, the tool is assigned to the Command button. So in Figure 2.9, I inserted pedal on/off events by choosing the Pedal On symbol, holding the Command key, and clicking where I want to place them. Logic Pro alternates the Pedal On/Off symbols automatically.

Figure 2.5   The Inspector in the Score Editor.

Figure 2.6   An mf symbol and a crescendo dragged into the Flute region.

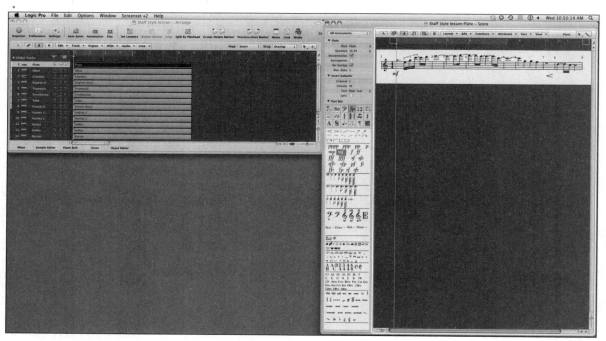

Figure 2.7   The crescendo symbol with its length and width adjusted.

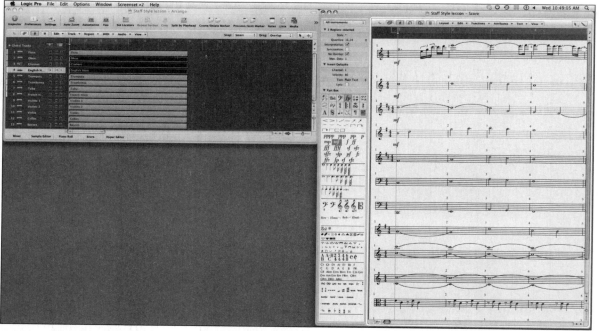

Figure 2.8   An mf symbol inserted simultaneously into multiple regions.

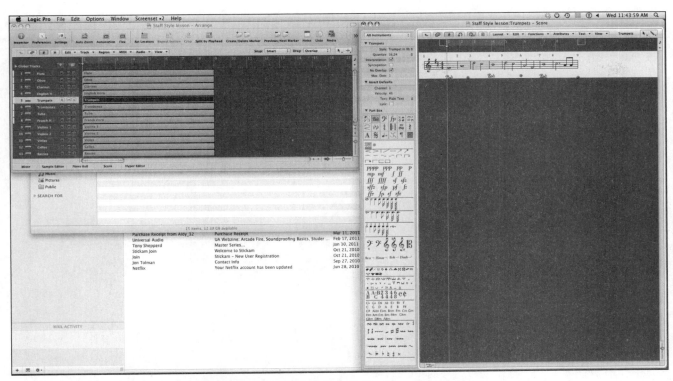

Figure 2.9 Pedal on/off events inserted with the Pencil tool.

For many tasks, however, my favorite way to enter symbols is via key command. In general, my rule with Logic Pro is to never do with a mouse what I can do with a keystroke. I almost always use key commands to insert staccatos, accents, crescendos, and diminuendos, among others.

1. Press Option-K to open the Key Commands Window. Search for staccato. In Figure 2.10, the Score Window shows no default keystroke assigned to Attach Symbol: Staccato. Presumably, you know how to assign a key command, but I will quickly do so here.

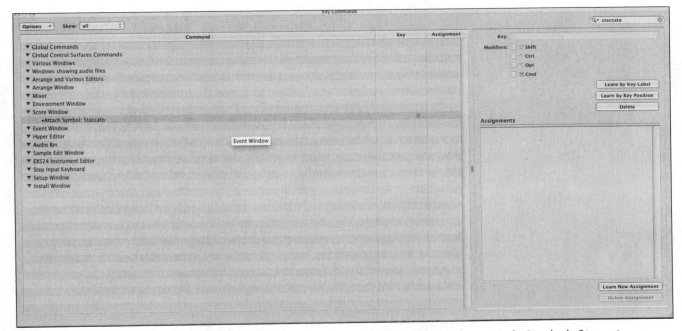

Figure 2.10 The Key Commands Window ready to assign a keystroke for Attach Symbol: Staccato.

2. Press Learn by Key Position (or Key Label) and press the period key on your keyboard. It is now learned. See Figure 2.11. Learn by Key Position is the better choice because, by default, the period key in the main part of the keyboard is assigned to "Forward." You will get a warning message that says, "Key or key combination already in use at lower priority," whereas the period or decimal point key in the 10-key keypad is unassigned.

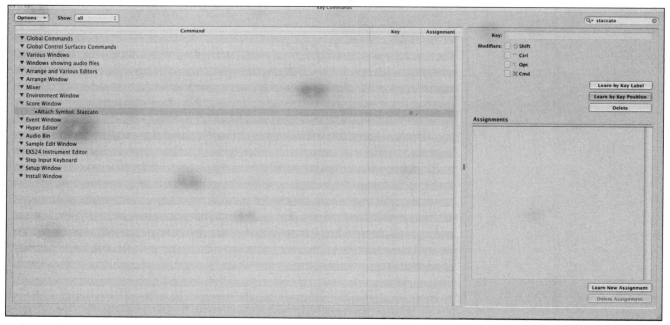

Figure 2.11 The Key Commands Window with an assigned keystroke for Attach Symbol: Staccato.

3. Press Learn by Key Position (or Key Label) again and close the Key Commands window.

4. Choose the Bass region, press Command-A to select all the notes, and press the period key. All the notes now have an attached staccato symbol, as you can see in Figure 2.12.

Figure 2.12 The bass region with notes with attached staccato symbols.

Note A word about MIDI meaning: I keep separate versions for how I want the notes to sound versus how they look, but Logic Pro does default to having MIDI meaning for some symbols (like Pedal On/Off) and provides the ability to assign MIDI meaning to others. Some when set, like accents, actually alter the MIDI data, while others, like the sustain pedal, do not. The Layout menu has a window where you can assign MIDI meaning to certain selected symbols. See Figures 2.13 and 2.14.

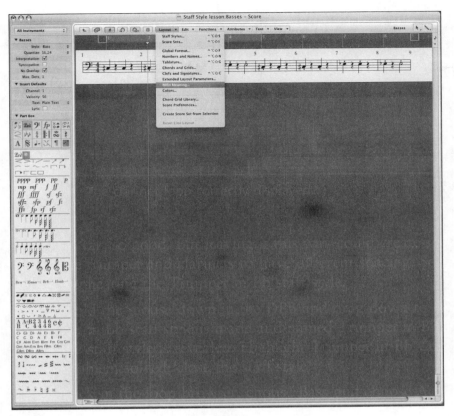

Figure 2.13 Accessing the MIDI Meaning Window.

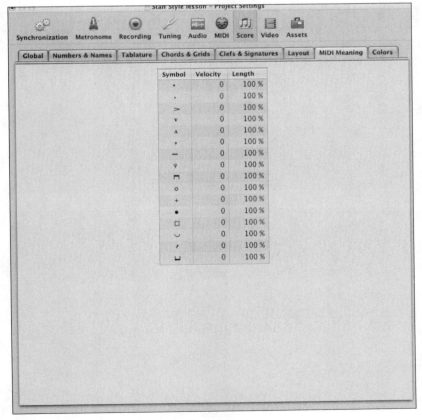

Figure 2.14 The MIDI Meaning Window.

3 Starting to Prepare Parts for Individual Instruments

You can approach this task several ways. In this chapter I will give you my favorite approach, plus some other ideas.

Assigning a Staff Style

You may want to assign a default staff style for each instrument in a template. However, I will assume you have not done so.

1. Create a new project with 10 software instruments, and select track 1.

2. Click the Display Parameter Box in the Inspector's disclosure triangle. You can see at the bottom that Style is set to Auto, as are all the tracks. See Figure 3.1.

3. You will use green Apple Loops to explore the principles of working with the staff styles. Navigate to the Media area in the loop browser and choose the Piano tab. Drag the green Apple Loop named 70s Ballad Piano 01 to the first track. Type N to open the integrated Score Editor (or open the standalone Score Editor by pressing Command-3). It should look like what you see in Figure 3.2.

4. Click in the Score Editor to make it the key focus. The yellow Show Content link should be on by default. If not, make sure it is on. In the Score Editor's Display Parameter Box, Auto correctly (*maybe*) chose Piano for the Style option. See Figure 3.3.

   There is a problem, however, with the default C3 split point. It determines which notes appear in the right and which appear in the left. Double-click the word Piano (next to Style) in the Display Parameter Box (DPB) to see the elements that it is comprised of. See Figure 3.4.

5. Double-click the C3 split and type F2. The notes in the left move to the right and looks the way a pianist wants to see it. Close the Piano style box, and you can see how it now appears in Figure 3.5.

   In many cases, no split points will work for the entre part. That is when you need to use a polyphonic staff style, which I will cover in a later tutorial. But for now, we will pronounce this good.

   Return to the loop browser, click Reset, and choose Bass and Relaxed.

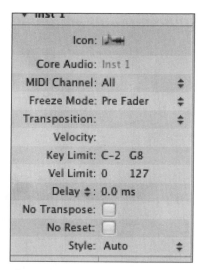

Figure 3.1 Style set to Auto in the Display Parameter Box.

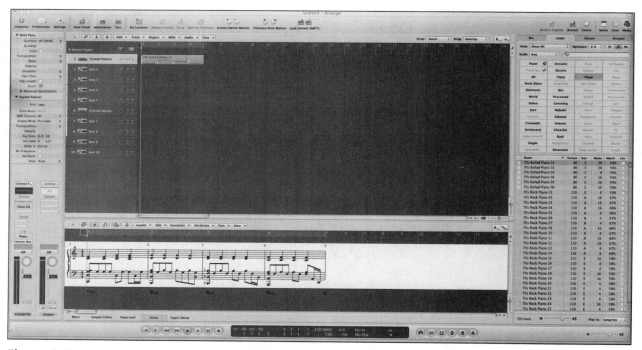

Figure 3.2 A piano loop in the Score Editor with the Staff Style set to Auto selected with the Same Level link engaged in the Score Editor.

Note   Disclaimer: The loops I am choosing make no musical sense at all, so for heaven's sake, don't listen to this.

---

6. Drag Southern Bass 01 to the second track. The Score Editor updates to show the bass loop's contents, and lo and behold, it has correctly assigned it to a Bass staff style. Pretty impressive, Logic Pro! Let's see how good you *really* are.

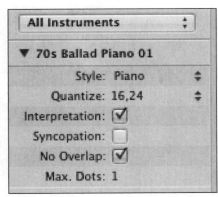

Figure 3.3 The Score Editor's Display Parameter Box showing that the loop is assigned to a Piano staff style.

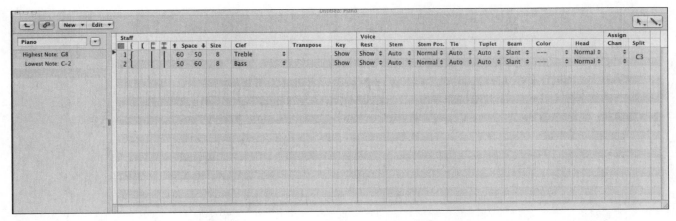

Figure 3.4 Inside the Piano staff set.

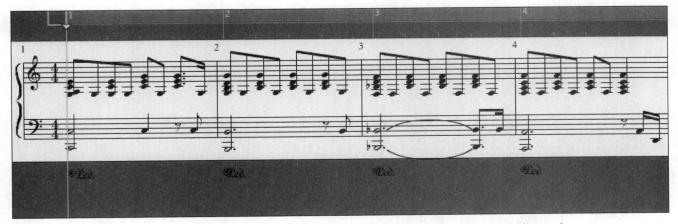

Figure 3.5 The piano loop in the Score Editor with the Piano style's split point adjusted.

7.   Back in the loop browser, click Reset and then type **clarinet** in the search field to bring up some choices, which you can see in Figure 3.6.

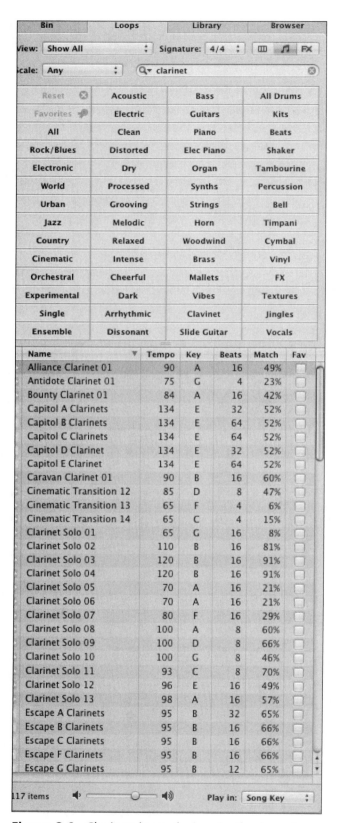

Figure 3.6 Clarinet loop choices in the loop browser.

8. Scroll down to Stormy A Clarinet and drag the loop to track 3. Click in the Score Editor to see that DPB Logic Pro has assigned it to a Treble staff style. Since the clarinet you most often will be writing for is a Bb transposing instrument, this will not work.

9. Hold the mouse down and scroll to choose the Trumpet in Bb staff style. Now it looks correct but the pitch is unchanged, which is what you want. See Figure 3.7.

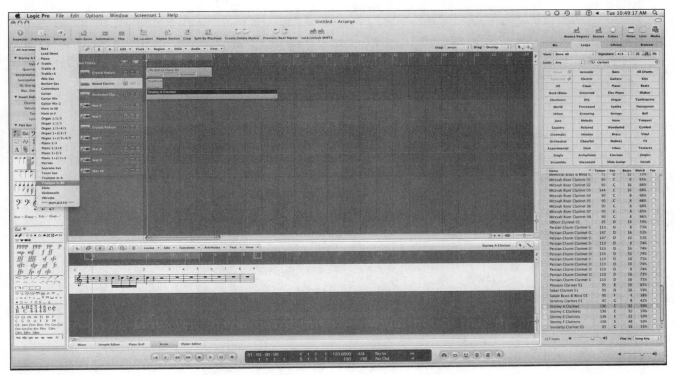

Figure 3.7   The clarinet loop correctly displayed.

So far, so good. But leaving it this way could create spacing issues later; you may want the trumpet and clarinets to have different spacing. So create a Clarinet staff style by duplicating the Trumpet in Bb staff style.

10. Hold the mouse down in the DPB and drag down to DUPLICATE. A copy of the Trumpet in Bb staff style is made and named Trumpet in Bb Copied. Double-click it, and again the staff style is revealed. Highlight Trumpet in Bb Copied and rename it Clarinet in Bb. Problem solved; close the staff style!

11. Back in the loop browser, choose Bass and choose Acoustic. Drag Cool Jazz Walking Bass 01 to track 4. Uh oh—Logic Pro did not do so well this time. It chose a Piano staff style when it should be Bass. No problem, right? Hold the mouse down on the Staff Style area and choose Bass. See Figure 3.8.

12. We still have a problem. It sounds right but it is displayed an octave too high. Using the methodology you employed earlier, duplicate and open the Bass staff style.

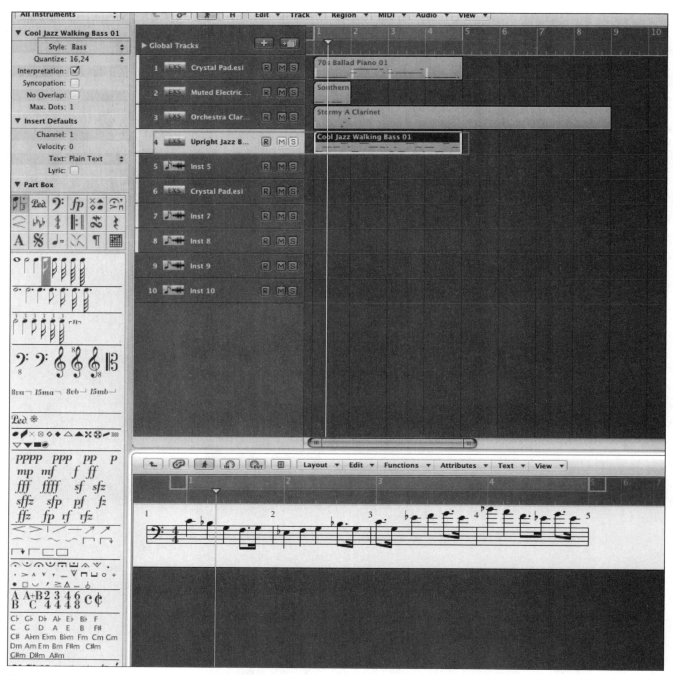

Figure 3.8 The bass loop assigned to the Bass staff style.

13. In the Transpose rectangle, double-click and type **–12** so that it displays an octave lower. Rename it Bass –8 and close it. The Bass now looks correct, as you can see in Figure 3.9.

    That was quite a lot of work! Ready for some good news? You can keep it in your templates—without saving the project with the loops/regions. Want some more good news? The staff styles you created can not only be saved in our templates but they can be imported from project to project.

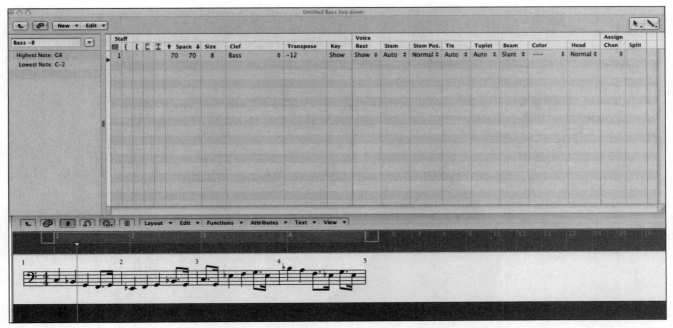

Figure 3.9 The bass loop assigned to the Bass staff style copied and adjusted to display an octave lower.

14. Close the Score Editor. In the Arrange Window's Instrument Parameter Box, assign the default staff style on track 1 to Piano, track 2 to Bass, track 3 to Clarinet in Bb, and track 4 to Bass −8.

15. Press Command-A to select all the loop regions and press Delete.

16. Using your keyboard's up and down arrows, scroll through the Track List. The default staff styles have been retained. See Figure 3.10.

17. Let's import the staff styles you created into a new project. Save the project to your desktop and name it Staff Style Lesson or something similar.

18. Press Command-N to open a new, empty project with four software instruments.

19. Go back to the Loop Browser in the Media area and again choose Bass and Acoustic. Find that same green Apple Loop named Cool Jazz Walking Bass 01.

20. Open the Score Editor. Where you select staff style in the Score Editor's DPB, hold down the mouse. Sadly, your Bass −8 staff style is not there. (Sniff.) Not to worry!

21. In the toolbar, click and hold Settings while you scroll down to Import Settings.

22. Navigate to the previously saved project. In the lower-right corner, click Import to bring up a bunch of available project settings.

23. Check only Staff Styles and then click Import. See Figure 3.11.

24. In the Score Editor's DPB, hold the mouse down and you can see that the Bass −8 staff style is available to select and assign to your bass loop in this new project.

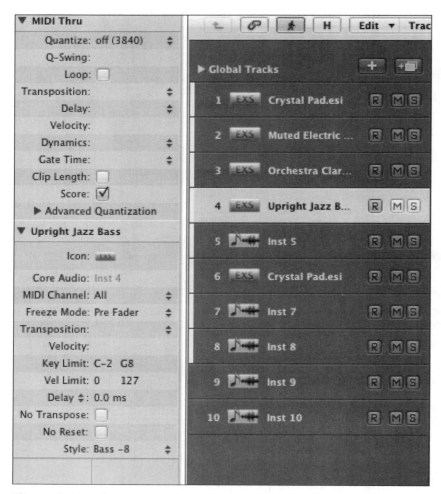

Figure 3.10 The acoustic bass track with the default staff style correctly retained.

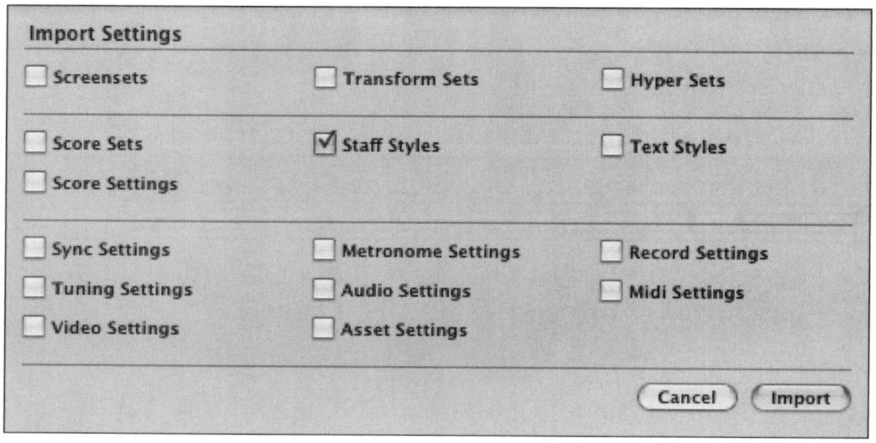

Figure 3.11 Import Settings choices.

So now you are familiar with the way most staff styles work. Once you get the hang of it, it is quite easy to create and import your own.

4 Display Quantization and Using Polyphonic Staff Styles Methods to Prepare Parts for Individual Instruments

Understanding Display Quantization

What you see in the Score Editor need not necessarily reflect that you have quantized regions in the Arrange Window or Piano Roll editor. The Score Editor's Display Quantization gives you the ability to have the notes display quantized, specifically for display at variance with how the part sounds with the actual quantization of MIDI events. In Figure 4.1, I have played in a swingy little piano part that sounds just right. However, traditionally swing music is notated as straight 8[th]s and that is how most players want to see it. Logic Pro defaults to having Interpretation on to make guesses regarding how the display should look—and it guesses correctly an amazing amount of the time, by the way. Maybe if I uncheck it? Oh, my: Look at Figure 4.2. That will not do at all! Re-check it.

The answer lies in the Display Quantization setting. Look again at Figure 4.1. The Score Editor's Display Parameter Box defaults to Quantize: 16,24. This affects display only and means that the Score Editor is assuming that the notes should be displayed with the smallest values up to 16th notes and 8th note triplets. That is not what you want, so you need to work with Display Quantization to get the part looking the way you actually want it to look.

1. Hold the mouse down and enter one of the following for Display Quantization: 8 or **8,12**. Looks good! See Figure 4.3.

2. The third box in the third row has a quarter note equal to a group. I look at the symbol choices in that group, and I see the perfect symbol to make clear that the player is seeing straight 8[th]s. It is actually to be played swing, which is an 8th triplet comprised of a quarter note and an 8th note. Drag it in to the region. Now it is correct. See Figure 4.4.

    But isn't swing music highly syncopated? I see that below the Interpretation check box is a Syncopation check box. Maybe it should be checked?

3. Check the Syncopation box just to see what it looks like (which is what you see in Figure 4.5). Is that what a player wants to see? The answer is no. A long time ago, jazz and pop/rock players found that if you allowed ties to cross an imaginary line across the middle of a measure, you were less likely to play it rhythmically correct; you should not do that in this case. Uncheck the Syncopation check box.

Figure 4.1   My little swing part in the Score Editor with its default settings.

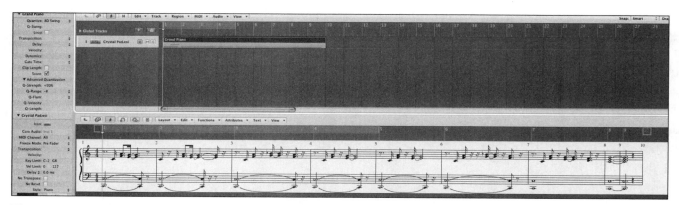

Figure 4.2   My little swing part in the Score Editor with Interpretation off.

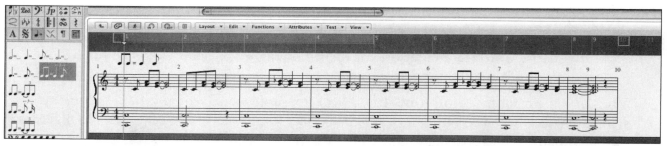

Figure 4.3   My little swing part in the Score Editor with the Display Quantization set to 8,12.

Figure 4.4   With the added Swing symbol.

Figure 4.5 With the Syncopation check box checked.

There will be times, however, when such settings will work for some figures but not for others. Fortunately, neither Interpretation or Syncopation is an all-or-nothing affair. You can check both or uncheck both. Override either option for certain notes; highlight the exception notes. Under the Attributes menu, you can choose Default, Force, or Defeat. See Figure 4.6.

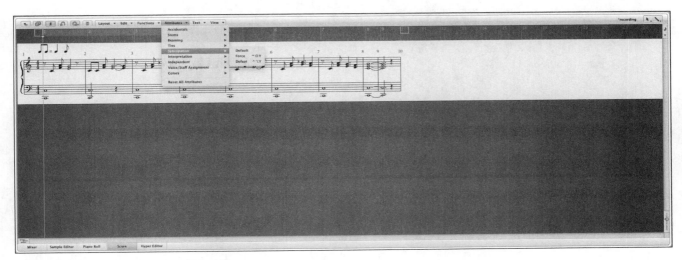

Figure 4.6 Syncopation options.

So far, so good. However, if you heard this you would notice that the middle Cs in bars 1–7, which appear as 8th notes, actually hold longer. There is no single split point that works. The answer is the Polyphonic staff style.

Using Polyphonic Staff Styles

Polyphonic staff styles are very powerful problem solvers. Logic Pro 9 comes with several already created.

1. In the Score Editor's Display Parameter Box (DPB), click the mouse and change Staff Style to Piano 1/3. This staff style assigns notes with an internal MIDI channel of 1 to the right hand and 3 to the left hand. Type **E** to open the Event List and see that all the notes in this region have the internal MIDI channel 1. They are all being displayed in the right hand. See Figure 4.7.

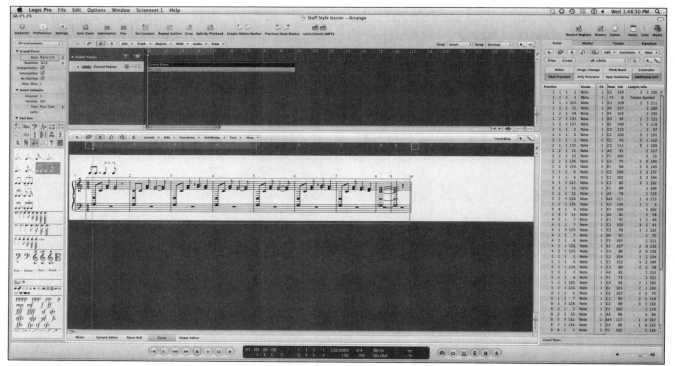

Figure 4.7 All the notes are being displayed for the right hand as they are all assigned to MIDI channel 1.

2. There are a couple of ways to deal with the splitting of notes between the right and left hands. One way is to rubber-band drag, or Shift-select, over all the notes that you want displayed in the left hand; in the Event List, double-click one note and type **3**. All the notes you selected now appear in the left hand. See Figure 4.8.

    This would be fine if the length of those middle Cs were reflected properly, but they are not. I need a three-voice Polyphonic staff style.

3. In the DPB, hold the mouse down and choose the staff style named Piano 1+2/3.

Figure 4.8   The Swing part assigned to the staff style Piano 1/3 with the notes for the left hand assigned to MIDI channel 3.

4. Select the first pesky middle C and press Shift-E for Select Equal objects. In the Event List, double-click a note and type **2**. Now we're talking! Polyphonic staff styles, baby! See Figure 4.9.

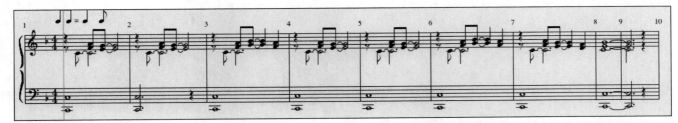

Figure 4.9   My piano part displayed correctly using the three-voice Polyphonic staff style named Piano 1+2/3.

Here is an example of a problem that is much easier to fix with a simpler Polyphonic staff style. I have played in another part in the key of F. I drag in the key of F indicator from the Part Box. (This makes every part in the project set to the key of F with transposed staff styles adjusted accordingly. To be clear: If I have played a trumpet part and assigned to it Trumpet in Bb staff style, it would be displayed in the key of G.) See Figure 4.10.

Figure 4.10   My second piano part, in the key of F.

5. I open the staff style and try to adjust the split point. No matter how you set it, it will not look the way a pianist wants to see it, because the melody is comprised of notes that sometimes are part of the left-hand accompaniment.

6. I change the staff style to Piano 1/3. Predictably, all the notes appear in the right because it is all MIDI channel 1 (as is clear in the Event List in Figure 4.11).

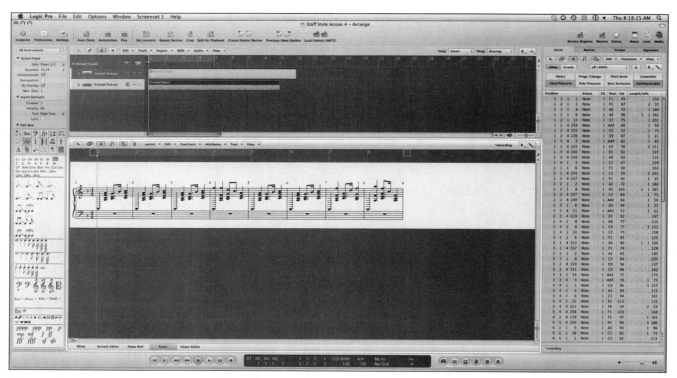

Figure 4.11 My second piano part assigned to the Piano 1/3 staff style.

7. I then click in the Score Editor to make sure it is the area of key focus. Press the Escape key to see the available Score Editor tools (shown in Figure 4.12). Notice that tool 7 is called Voice Separation, which I then choose.

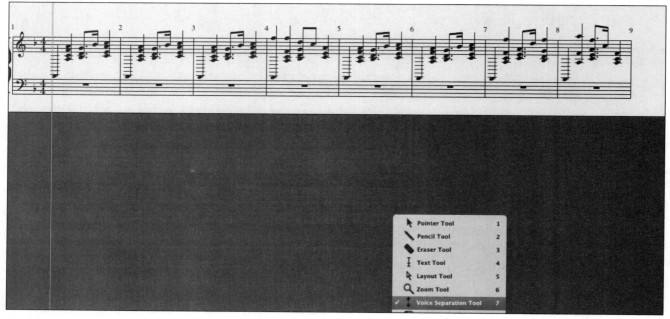

Figure 4.12 Choosing the Voice Separation tool.

8. I can now simply draw around the notes I wish to be displayed in the left hand, as you see in Figure 4.13. The Voice Separation tool assigns the notes to MIDI Channel 3 in the Piano 1/3 staff style. If some notes end up in the wrong hand, it is simple to draw under or over the errant notes. The end result is reflected in Figure 4.14.

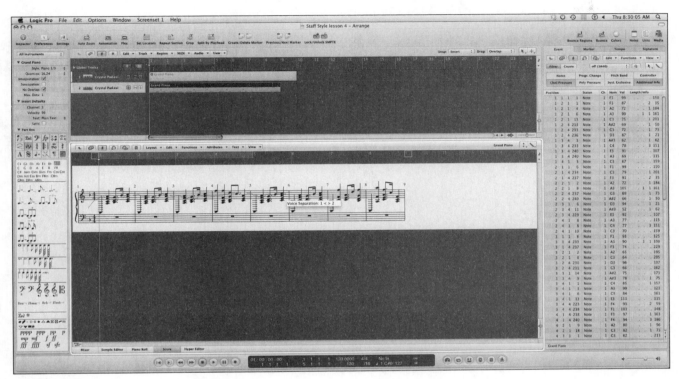

Figure 4.13 Using the Voice Separation tool.

Figure 4.14 The end result after using the Voice Separation tool.

5 More Display Quantization Techniques and Triplet/ Tuplet Display

More on Display Quantization

In Figure 5.1, you can see a little phrase I played in real time on a Celtic Tin Whistle patch, in Eb. I have left it un-quantized, presumably either because I like the way it sounds or because it is only for printout purposes.

Let's do some more exploring.

1. Uncheck the Interpretation check box to see what I actually played (instead of what the Score Editor assumes I meant to play). No flautist wants to see that, so re-check the Interpretation check box.

2. Open the Event List and select the last four notes. Unless I meant these notes to be very syncopated, the problem is evident: They are quite late. See Figure 5.2.

3. With the four notes still selected, double-click the first note. Change the last entry in the position columns from 140 to 14. It looks better, as you can see in Figure 5.3. (Alternatively, you can use the Quantize tool.)

4. Check Syncopation to see if it helps the part at all. The only change is in the first measure, and it does not solve the issue of its readability; uncheck Syncopation. Uncheck Note Overlap; it is clear that my playing was a little sloppy, so thank you to Logic Pro for helping. Re-check Note Overlap. (You will almost always want Note Overlap checked. It is far better to deal with an overlapped note display with a Polyphonic staff style, as explained in Tutorial 4. Max dots should be self-explanatory; adjustments are required only for doubly and triply dotted notes.)

5. You could move the MIDI position of the last two notes in bar 1 as I did earlier, but perhaps choosing the correct Display Quantization setting will solve this. As there are both 16th notes (16) and 8th note triplets in this phrase (12), you need a hybrid setting. Choose 16/12 in the Display Parameter Box. Now the part looks exactly the way a player wants to see it. See Figure 5.4.

Figure 5.1 The Celtic Tin Whistle part in the Score Editor with its default settings.

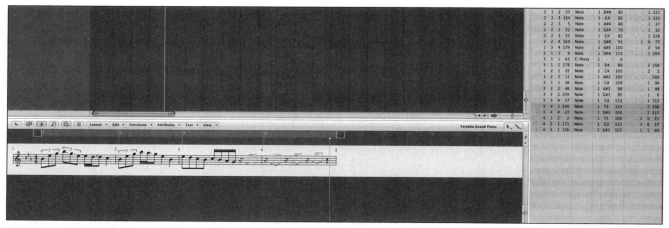

Figure 5.2 The same part also visible in the Event List.

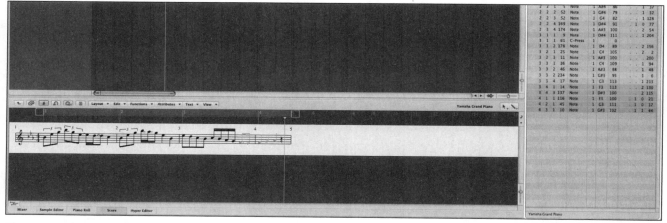

Figure 5.3 The same part with the actual MIDI position of the last four notes corrected in the Event List.

Figure 5.4 The Celtic Tin Whistle phrase properly displayed.

When Defeat Interpretation Doesn't Work

Most of the time, you want Interpretation on. You can defeat it for certain notes by opening the Attributes menu, as explained in Tutorial 4. Double-clicking a single note shows the Note Attributes Window, which allows you to make multiple display decisions. See Figure 5.5.

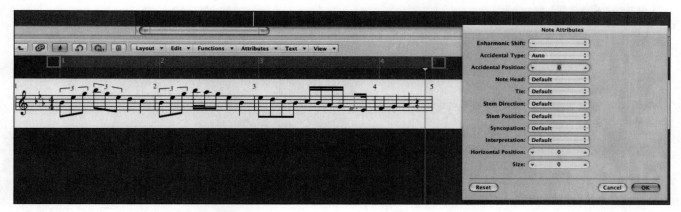

Figure 5.5 The Note Attributes Window.

But sometimes this still does not bring the result you want. Look at Figure 5.6; what you see displayed as a whole note is actually 3½ beats long. But because Interpretation is on, it assumes I want a whole note. It looks incorrect even after I defeat Interpretation, as you can see in Figure 5.7.

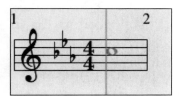

Figure 5.6 The 3½ beat long note with Interpretation on, displayed as a whole note.

Figure 5.7 The 3½ beat long note with Interpretation off, displayed as a dotted half note tied to a quarter note.

The solution is to insert a user rest at the proper break point.

1. Click the quarter note rest symbol in the tool box to reveal the Rests palette.

2. Select the 8th note rest and drag it into the region while keeping an eye on the help tag (precisely at the last 8th note position in the measure—in this case, 1 4 3 1). It's better, as you can see in Figure 5.8. But what about the "no tie over the imaginary middle of the bar" rule?

3. Drag a quarter note rest into the region at 1 3 1 1. Finally it looks right; see Figure 5.9.

It is a testament to human adaptability that over time, working like this no longer seems odd after a while!

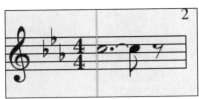

Figure 5.8 The 3½ beat long note with Interpretation off displayed as a dotted half note tied to an 8th note, followed by an 8th rest.

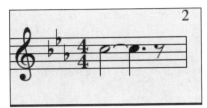

Figure 5.9 The note corrected so that it does not tie over the imaginary middle of the bar.

Triplets and Tuplets

This is Logic Pro's version of "Lions and tigers and bears, oh my!"

Logic automatically displays triplets properly if you have played them reasonably accurately (or have quantized the MIDI in the Arrange Window or Piano Roll and Event editors, as in Figure 5.10). But there are times, especially when rests are in the triplet/tuplet, where the part's display becomes problematic. Check out Figure 5.11. The solution is the n-tuplet symbol.

Figure 5.10 Well-played and/or quantized triplets.

Figure 5.11 Triplets with nested rests.

1. In the Part Box, click the 3 next to the 8th note in the very first square; then choose the n-tuplet symbol. See Figure 5.12.

2. Drag the n-tuplet symbol into the region right over the first note of beat 2. The menu appears that you see in Figure 5.13. In this case, the default setting is correct. (It's three

8th triplet notes taking place in the amount of time that two 8th notes usually do. Duh, Jay! Isn't that what an 8th note triplet is?) But it is not what you want (within the triplet an 8th note, 8th rest, and 8th note). See Figure 5.14.

3. Double-click that note and defeat Interpretation. Now you have what you want. Do the same procedure for beat 4 of that measure. So far, so good, as you can see in Figure 5.15.

Here is where is starts to get a little hairy. The third beat of bar 2 should be a triplet beginning with a nested 8th rest followed by a ¼ note. If I try to insert the n-tuplet symbol at 2 2 1 1, however, the Score Editor simply will not let me do it. *(Bad Score Editor, bad!)*

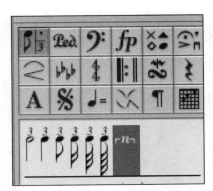

Figure 5.12   Choosing the n-tuplet symbol.

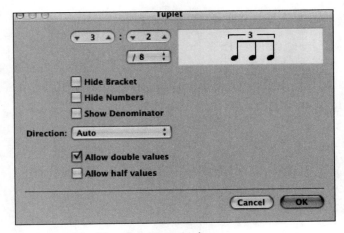

Figure 5.13   The Tuplet Window.

Figure 5.14   Bar 1 correctly displayed.

Figure 5.15 Measure 1 correctly displayed.

4. Insert an 8th rest at 2 3 1 1.

5. Drag the n-tuplet symbol over that 8th rest.

6. Beat 4 should be a triplet with an 8th note, 8th rest, and 8th note. Drag the n-tuplet symbol over the first note of beat 4 and defeat Interpretation for that note.

    It has been, as they say in Yiddish, a little bit of a *potchke* (fuss, bother), but what you see in Figure 5.16 is what the player should see.

Figure 5.16 The whole phrase correctly displayed.

Obviously, triplets are not the only kind of tuplets. In Figure 5.17, you can see a flute run I played in real time. The first seven notes should begin on the fourth beat of bar 1, ending with the high C on the downbeat of bar 2. I could quantize and move MIDI notes around, but since this is for printout, here is where the n-tuplet shines.

Figure 5.17 The flute run played in real time.

7. Select all the notes in the run except for the first and last notes; delete them. Make sure the two remaining notes are in the proper MIDI position.

8. Drag the n-tuplet over the first note. In the window, set it for seven 16th notes over the time that four would normally occur. See Figure 5.18. It now looks like what you see in Figure 5.19.

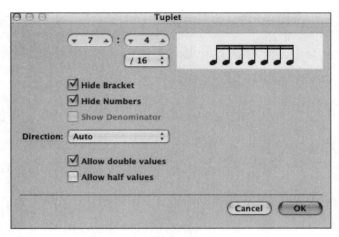

Figure 5.18   The n-tuplet window.

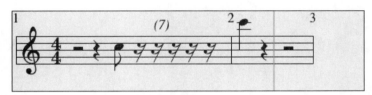

Figure 5.19   The edited flute run.

9.   The first note is too long, so turn off Interpretation and shorten it in the Event List. You can also change the duration in the Piano Roll, in the Score Editor's Display Parameter Box, or via duration bars in the Score Editor (more on that later). You should see what is displayed in Figure 5.20.

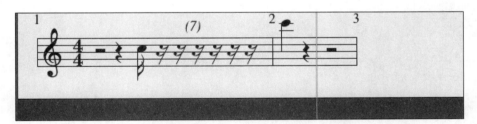

Figure 5.20   The flute run further edited for tuplets.

10.   Using the Pencil tool, select a 16th note tuplet member from the Part Box's palette. Pencil in the desired notes, adjusting them for any errors. Attach and adjust a slur and an accent. You can see the end result in Page View in Figure 5.21. (The 7 you see in parentheses will not print, by the way.)

Nested tuplets and triplets are a problem in Logic Pro. In theory, the Score Editor cannot do them. In reality, it can. In Figure 5.22, I have tried to play a triplet with two quarter notes and then two 8th notes in a nested triplet. If I drag the triplet sign over the first note, I get the

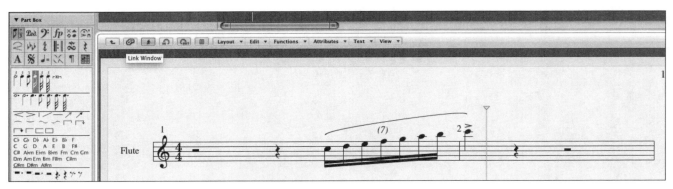

Figure 5.21 The flute run finished in Page View.

unacceptable result that you see in Figure 5.23. If, however, I use the Hide Number setting and choose Allow Double Values, shown in Figure 5.24, I get a result that I can live with by using the Text tool to create and put a 3 over it, selecting the Tuplet Text Style so that it is visually consistent with the 3s in the other triplets, as you see in Figure 5.25.

Figure 5.22 The nested triplet played in real time with the default display.

Figure 5.23 The nested triplet with a triplet n-tuplet.

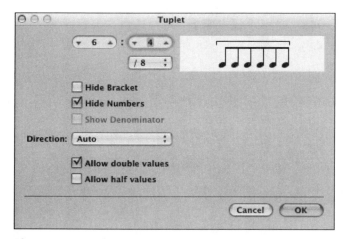

Figure 5.24 The nested triplet workaround for n-tuplet settings.

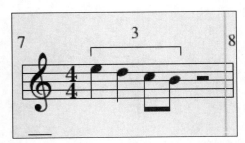

Figure 5.25 The nested triplet properly, if inelegantly, displayed.

In *The Logic Notation Guide*, Johannes Prischl describes this as the "Quick and Dirty Solution" and then offers a more elegant—but much more time-consuming—method using a Polyphonic staff style. I would include the solution if this book's focus were engraved quality scores for publishing, but the solution you created in this tutorial is fine for parts and scores for recording sessions. It poses no clarity problem for the player.

6 Grace Notes, Beamed Grace Notes, and Other Problematic Issues for Parts

Grace Notes: Single and Beamed

In Figure 6.1, you can see I have played a series of grace notes followed by longer notes. Making these notes look right is no problemo.

1. Select the notes that you want displayed as grace notes. Under the Score Editor's Attributes menu, choose Independent > Independent Grace. They all are displayed as 8th notes with a slash, as is traditional. See Figure 6.2.

2. Open the event list, select the main notes, and move them onto the beat. You could quantize them. The problem is that they are displayed on top of each other. See Figure 6.3.

    If you look in the upper-right corner of this screenshot, you will see that the Score Editor has defaulted to the Pencil tool. Hold the mouse down and scroll to the Layout tool. After all your notes have been entered, Layout is the most valuable tool in the Score Editor.

3. With the notes still selected, hold the Command key and move the notes to the right with the Layout tool. The results look like what you see in Figure 6.4. Easy as pie!

    Displaying grace notes beamed together is another task that you have to trick the Score Editor into displaying properly. Figure 6.5 shows what I have played in this example. Bar 1 should begin with two grace notes and bar 2 with three, but they will not be beamed together if I use the same method I used for the single grace notes; there is no way to do so directly. Once again, the Polyphonic staff style is your friend. This time you will create your own. Remember: You can import these styles from project to project; you may eventually want to keep them in a template.

4. Duplicate the Treble staff style and open the copy. Rename the style **Treble for beamed grace notes**.

5. Under the New menu, choose Insert Voice. A second line appears. In Staff Style under Assign, assign the first voice to channel 1 and the second voice to channel 16. Hide the rests in the second voice in the Rest column; choose Up in the Stem column. See Figure 6.6.

6. Close the staff style. Under the Score Editor's View menu, check Explode Polyphony. A second empty staff appears, as you can see in Figure 6.7.

Figure 6.1 A flute part in the Score Editor with its default settings.

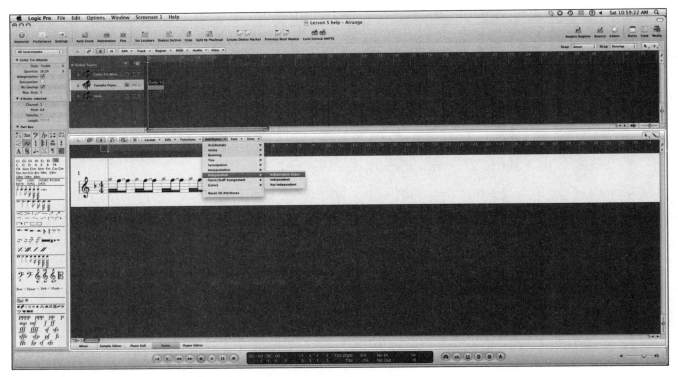

Figure 6.2 The same part with independent grace notes.

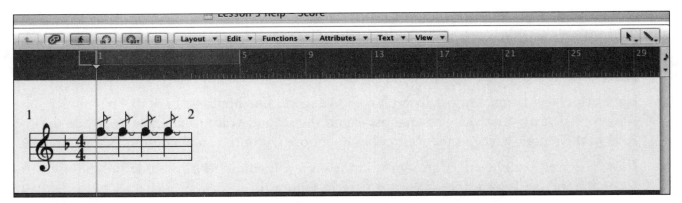

Figure 6.3 The notes displayed on top of each other after adjusting their position.

Figure 6.4 The primary notes are properly displayed with the grace notes after being moved with the Layout tool.

Figure 6.5 A flute part that needs a beamed grace note display.

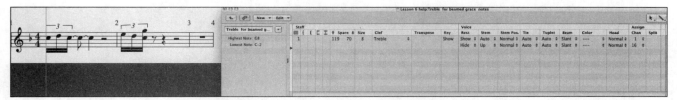

Figure 6.6 A Polyphonic staff style configured to help achieve a properly beamed grace note display.

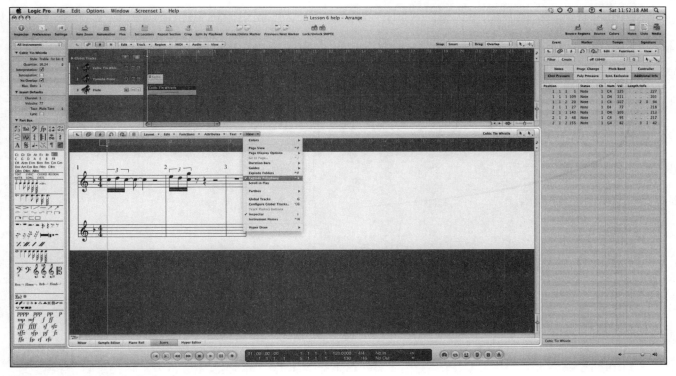

Figure 6.7 Explode Polyphony.

7. Assign the intended grace notes to MIDI channel 16. They jump down to the lower staff.

8. Move the notes in the upper staff to their proper position. See Figure 6.8.

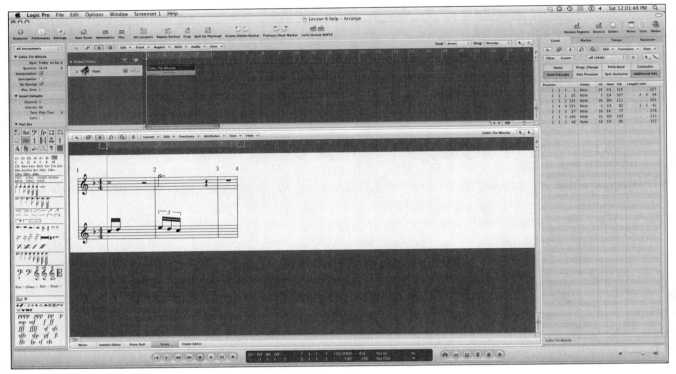

Figure 6.8 Notes in the two staffs properly positioned.

9. Highlight the notes in the lower staff, press the Esc key, and choose tool 0 (Resize). Size the notes to taste. (I made them smaller in this case, with –8.) The result looks like Figure 6.9. Press the Esc key twice to return to the Pointer tool.

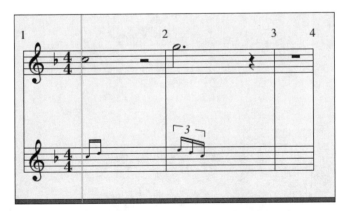

Figure 6.9 The beamed grace notes resized.

10. Hold the Command key and adjust the notes' display on the two staffs. See Figure 6.10.

Figure 6.10   After the Layout tool work.

11.   Under the View menu, uncheck Explode Polyphony. Hallelujah, you have beamed grace notes! See Figure 6.11.

Figure 6.11   Beamed grace notes.

You can create cue notes in a similar fashion with a Polyphonic staff style for players who need to see, for example, what a singer sings before the player enters. Explode Polyphony would not be needed for this task.

Pickup Bars

The correct term for pickup bars is actually *anacrusis*, but frankly I have never heard anyone in the world of commercial music call them that. You can clearly see in Figure 6.12 that I have played in a part that has a pickup, but it played starting on the fourth beat of bar 1. I want the downbeat of bar 2 to actually be the downbeat of bar 1. Dealing with this is pretty simple.

Figure 6.12   A part that clearly has a pickup.

1.   Adjust the start time of the Logic Pro project by grabbing the Project Start rectangle in the upper part of the bar ruler (in this case, to 0 4 1 1). (You may have to hold down the Control key to get it to that precise position.) See Figure 6.13.

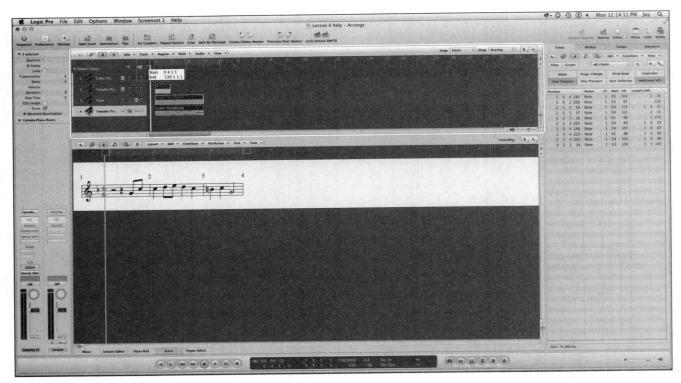

Figure 6.13 Adjusting the project start position.

2. Grab the lower left end of the region and drag its beginning to 0 4 1 1, as I am doing in Figure 6.14.

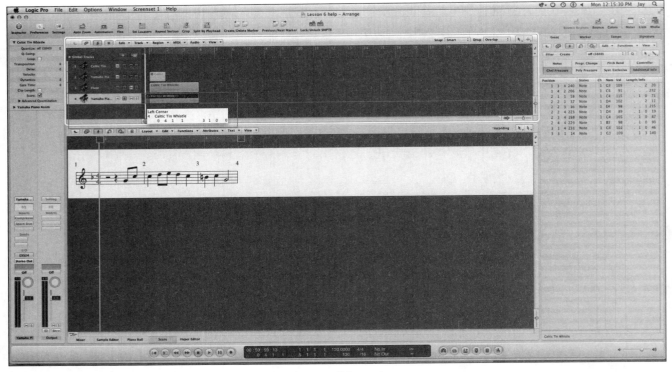

Figure 6.14 Changing the region's start position and length.

3. In the editor of your choice, select all the notes and move them so that the first note in the region is placed at 0 4 1 1. In Figure 6.15, you now have successfully created a pickup leading into bar 1.

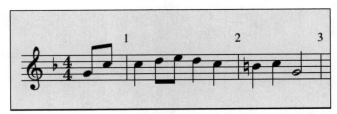

Figure 6.15 A part that has a pickup leading into bar 1.

7 Working with Score Sets, Symbols, and Note Alteration

Creating and Customizing Score Sets

Score sets are a very powerful feature of Logic Pro's Score Editor, and they are not only for printout but for editing and inserting symbols and other markings. That is why I discuss them this early in the book. Good use of score sets can save you a lot of time.

In Figure 7.1, you can see an excerpt of a MIDI file for a piece called "Water Music" by an up-and-coming composer named Georg Friedrich Handel. Notice the default non-editable score set, All Instruments, in the upper-left corner. If you double-click on it to open its window, you get see a message telling you just that, that the default All Instruments Set is not editable.

1. Press Command-A in the Score Editor to select all the regions. Under the Layout menu, choose Create Score Set from Selection. See Figure 7.2.

2. A score set with unwieldy abbreviations of the instrument names has been created. Under the View menu, check Page View. Again under the View menu, uncheck Instrument Names. Zoom out by holding Control-Option-up arrow. The result is shown in Figure 7.3.

3. Instrument names are only on page 1. Double-click the score set to open it and see your options. See Figure 7.4.

4. Click the name and type in **Full Score**. Scale and Format settings are right below the name. Scale is 100% and, because not a lot of instruments are in this piece, I do not need to scale it down. With a large orchestral piece, frequently I have to go as low as 55%. Before you make any such decisions, however, make sure that you have selected the proper paper size in the Page Setup window so that you have an accurate depiction of how it will be printed out. I print out my full scores on 8.5 x 14, or Legal size as it commonly is referred to.

   If you click Format, it changes from Score to Part so you have different Scale settings for parts and full score. Personally, I find this useless. Because I print parts and scores on different size paper, I keep a separate project for each.

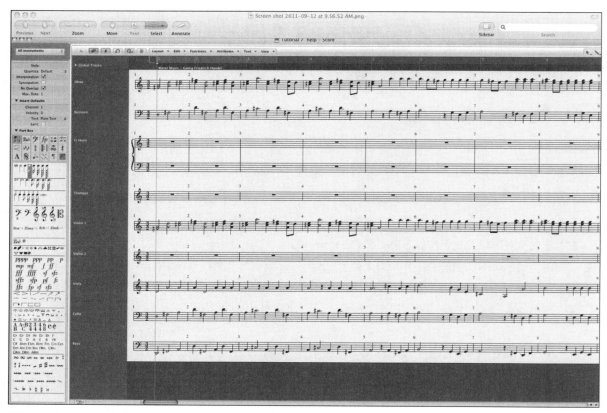

Figure 7.1 Handel's "Water Music" MIDI file excerpt.

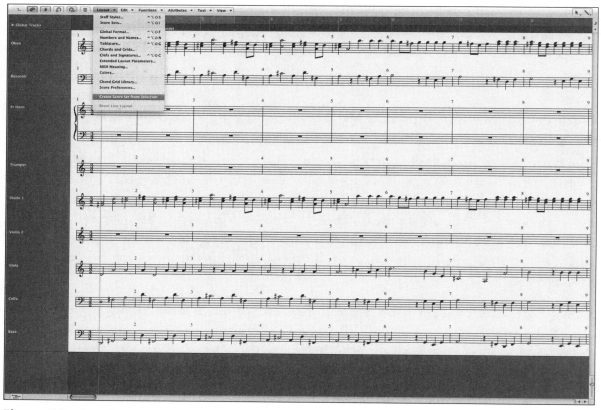

Figure 7.2 Creating a score set.

Figure 7.3   The newly created score set in Page View.

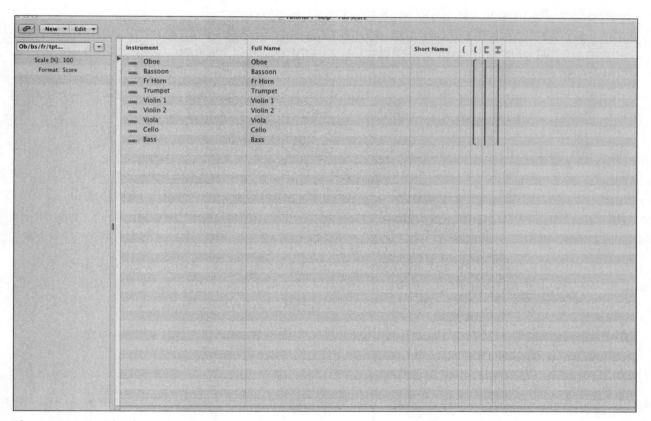

Figure 7.4   Inside the score set.

Figure 7.5 Page View with long names on page 1 and short names on subsequent pages.

5. Type in a short name for each instrument; they appear in all the pages following page 1. See Figure 7.5.

6. Close the score set. Under the Score Editor's View menu, uncheck Page View to return to Linear View for what I wish to show you next.

Entering Symbols in Linear View

Some symbols, like time and key, affect every part in the project; dragging them into a region is effectively the same as dragging them to multiple regions. Most symbols, like dynamics and accents, do not. Some, like trills, are independent and can be placed anywhere; others, like staccatos and accents, attach to notes.

Fortunately, Logic Pro's Score Editor lets you do multiple insertions or multiple attachments at a time in a score set. (What you do next has no musical validity in terms of Mr. Handel's intentions; I'm just illustrating methods. My deepest apology to Mr. Handel.)

1. Shift-select the bottom five tracks in the Arrange Window and create a new score set.

2. Open the score set and rename it **Strings**. Now you see only the strings in the Score Editor. See Figure 7.6.

Figure 7.6 The Strings score set.

3. Shift-select all but Violin 2, which does not enter at bar 1. Choose the symbol for mezzo-forte, and while pressing Shift and keeping an eye on the help tag, drag it to the bottom staff at bar 1.

4. Add crescendos at bar 5 and forte at bar 6 in the same manner.

5. On the downbeat of bar 6, add the tr symbol for trills and drag it to the right for the proper length. See Figure 7.7. Using the key commands assigned to staccato and accents, rubber-band (drag the mouse over) the desired notes and add them. Finally, add repeat signs for bars 1–12. These do not cause Logic Pro to repeat the section on playback, sadly. Also, they are global symbols and so will appear in every score set. You can see the result of all this in Figure 7.8.

I think you can now see just how powerful score sets are. You can create a whole bunch of these for editing and print purposes and either save them with your templates or import them from a project in which they exist. They are extremely helpful.

Sometimes the Score Editor makes some questionable choices about where it places things like accents or fermatas; you may want to make your own choices. I added accents to the

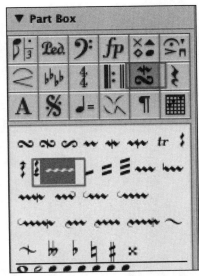

Figure 7.7 The adjustable trill symbol.

Figure 7.8 The Strings score set with dynamics, trills, staccatos, and accents added.

three lower string parts at bar 7. In the cello part, it looks correct, above the note, but in the viola and bass parts, I think it should be above the note. The key command will not be helpful here because you need to insert user accents, which, like all user symbols, allow you to reposition them; the standard symbols do not.

6. Delete the two accents and Shift-select the viola and bass parts.

7. Hold the Option key and select the accent note extension; while still pressing the Option key, press Shift. Now you can insert them below the notes. See Figure 7.9.

Figure 7.9 Attaching user accents.

Spend some serious time experimenting with all the independent symbols, note extensions, and global symbols that Logic Pro provides. It is an impressive palette!

Enharmonics, Beaming, Force Legato, and Note Overlap Correction

Logic Pro's Score Editor is a pretty good guesser based on any key you have entered, but (again) it may not make the enharmonic choices that you think are best for the player. In Figure 7.10, some B flats are followed by B naturals, so I think it would be better if the B flats were displayed as A sharps.

1. Select a Bb in the part. Under the Edit menu, choose Select Similar Events. All B flats are highlighted. Under the Attributes menu, choose Accidental > Enharmonic Shift #. Now all are displayed as A sharps. See Figures 7.11 and 7.12.

Figure 7.10 A part in need of enharmonic alteration.

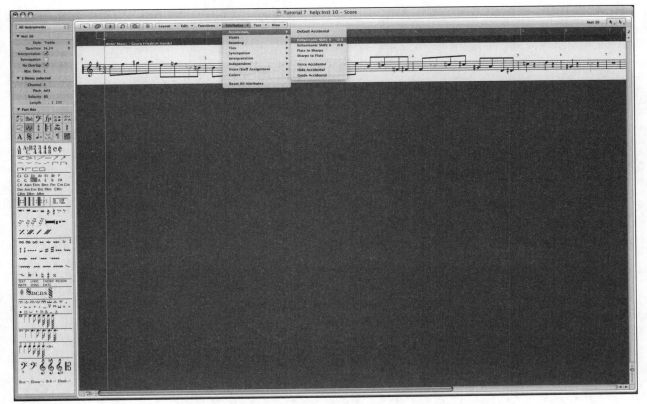

Figure 7.11 Enharmonic shifting in the Attributes menu.

Figure 7.12 The B flats are now A sharps.

Here is a valuable lesson I learned years ago when I first started doing score preparation work for composer and fellow Logic Pro user David Michael Frank. If you look at this example in the last quarter note of bar 3, you see an F sharp followed by an F natural followed by another F sharp on the first beat of bar 4. Because you are in the key of D Major, technically no sharps need be displayed. However, David suggested using a Force Accidental in that situation because if players are coming after the F natural, there is a good chance they will play the next note natural. I said, "Really? These L.A. studio musicians are some of the finest in the world; surely that will not happen." He replied, "Wait and see." He was right; they played the wrong note.

2. Highlight the two F sharps and navigate to the Attributes menu; choose Accidentals > Force Accidental, as shown in Figure 7.13. Of course, in this specific case, you could avoid the issue by changing the F natural enharmonically to E sharp.

Now let's deal with the beaming issues. The Score Editor has defaulted to beaming four 8th notes together, but you want to see them in groups of two.

3. In bar 1, highlight the second, third, fifth, and sixth notes.

4. Under the Edit menu, choose Select Equal Subpositions. See Figure 7.14.

5. Under the Attributes menu, navigate to Beaming > Unbeam Selected, as shown in Figure 7.15. Now it is the way you want it to be. See Figure 7.16.

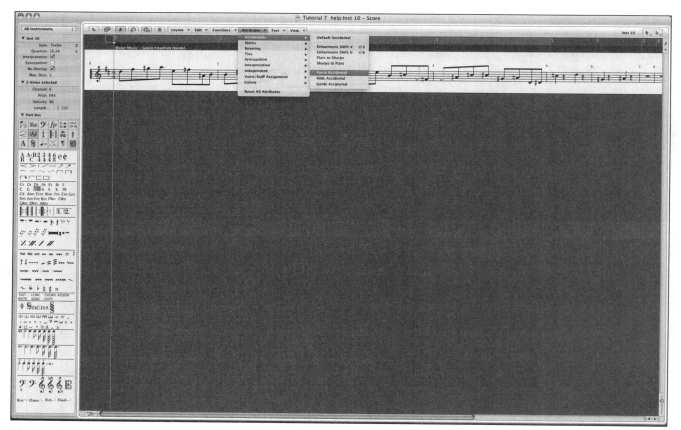

Figure 7.13 Using Force Accidental to be safe.

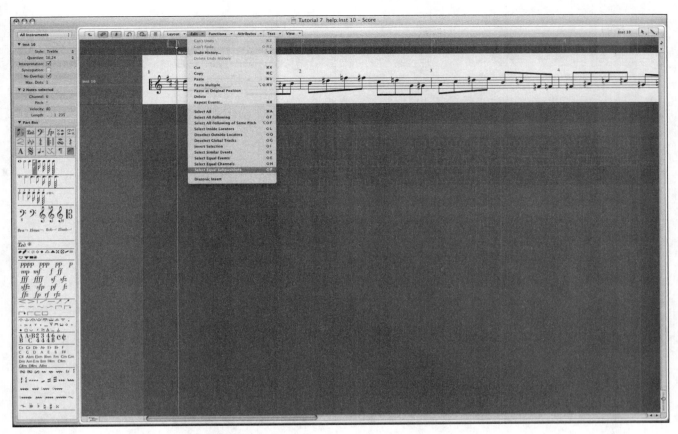

Figure 7.14 Select Equal Subpositions.

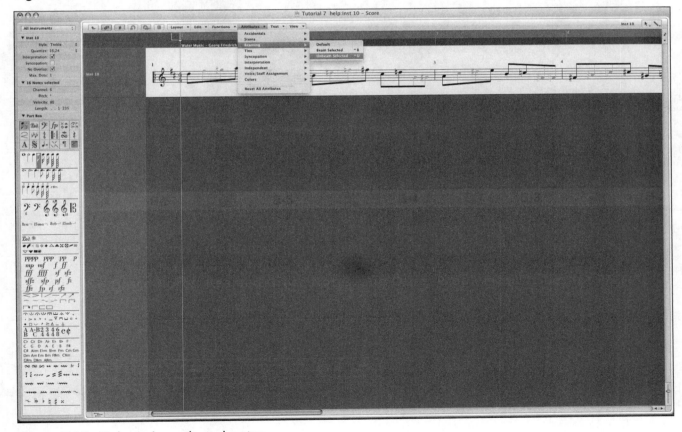

Figure 7.15 Unbeaming selected notes.

Figure 7.16   The notes are now beamed in groups of two rather than four.

The Force Legato and Note Overlap Correction choices in the Functions menu generally affect the sound of the MIDI rather than the display, but in this example's bars 5 and 6, there are four quarter notes that should have been half notes, connecting to the whole note in bar 8. Highlight them and navigate to the Functions menu; then choose Note Events > Note Force Legato (selected/selected). You get the desired result of four half notes connected to a whole note. See Figure 7.17.

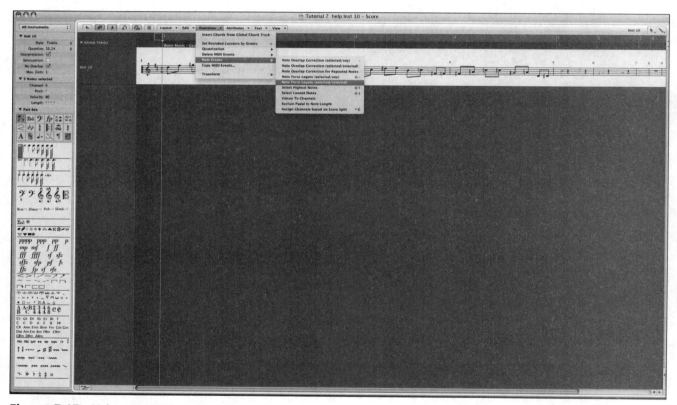

Figure 7.17   Using Note Force Legato.

8 Working with Lyric Entry, Text Styles, Headers, and Footers

Entering Lyrics

Entering your lyrics is a pretty straightforward affair in Logic Pro. In Figure 8.1, you can see that I have chosen the text group in the Part Box and then, just below it, Lyric.

Lyric entry is best done in Linear View, in my opinion, as there are fewer page redraws, and your eyes need not keep readjusting horizontally.

1. Drag the Lyric entry into the Score Editor under the first note while keeping an eye on the help tag. See Figure 8.2.

2. Type in the correct syllable and press the Tab key to the next note. Keep doing the same until the end. The result is shown in Figure 8.3. Notice that I use hyphenation to divide words that are sung over multiple notes. Similarly, a hyphen alone can be used to indicate a syllable or word, like *I*, that is held over multiple notes. If you accidentally hit the Return or Enter key, you will exit the text entry mode. You can resume by again dragging the word *Lyric* from the Part Box or using the Pencil tool.

3. Unfortunately, I messed up approximately in bar 5; I didn't allow for the fact that the word *I* is held over two notes. I had to make up for that by manually moving the following syllables to the correct positions, and now it is a bit of a mess. The syllables need to be aligned vertically.

4. No problem, right? Select a syllable and press Shift-E for Select Equal Events or rubber-band select them. Under the Text menu, choose Align and look for something like Align Vertically. But there is nothing of the sort there! See Figure 8.4.

5. Here is where certain key command-only functions come into play. They are helpful not only for lyrics but for other symbol and text-alignment tasks. Press Option-K to open the Key Commands Window. Type **align** in the search area and select Align Object Positions Vertically, as shown in Figure 8.5. You will see that there is no default key command assigned.

6. Using Learn by Key Position, assign it to Ctrl-Option-Command-V. Also assign Control-Option-Command-H to Align Object Positions Horizontally, which will be useful later on. See Figure 8.6.

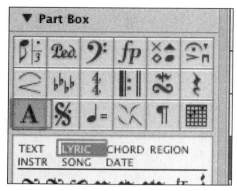

Figure 8.1 Lyric from the Part Box selected.

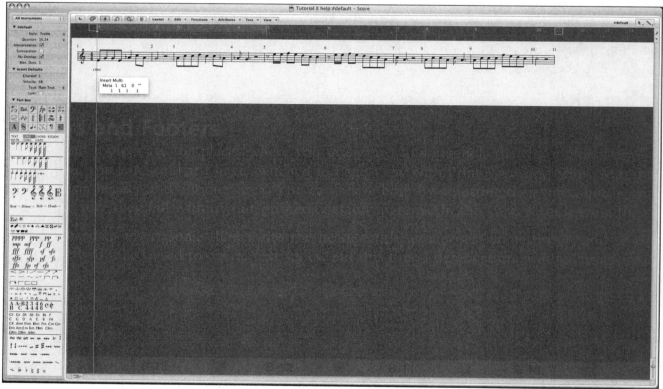

Figure 8.2 Entering lyrics.

Figure 8.3 Lyrics entered, though with some issues.

Figure 8.4 Results of alignment choices made in the Text menu.

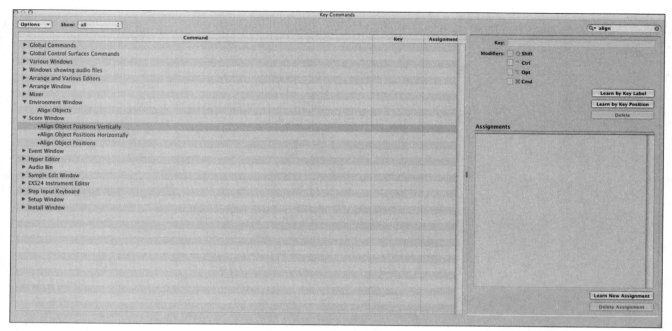

Figure 8.5 Align Object Positions Vertically in the Key Commands Window.

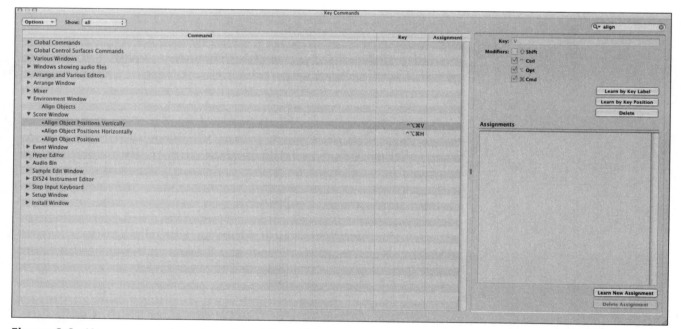

Figure 8.6 Key commands assigned to Align Object Positions Vertically and Horizontally in the Key Commands Window.

7. With all the syllables still selected, use the key command to tweak the displayed position a little with the Layout tool, and it is looking good in Figure 8.7.

    You may need to do further adjusting in Page View when printing the parts, but for now, so far, so good.

Figure 8.7 The lyrics, aligned and adjusted with the Layout tool.

Creating Text Styles

Everyone has his own idea of how text should look for things like the title, composer's credit, directions, articulation, and instructions. The defaults in different score programs vary somewhat. I have no real dog in that hunt. For me, as long as the words are clear, obvious, and neat, they are valid. I have learned from experience, however, that a less-is-more approach to font choices makes for cleaner scores and parts.

Unfortunately, Logic's Score Editor text-style creation process got a little more cumbersome in the transition from Logic Pro 7 to Logic Pro 8. Under the Text menu, choose Text Styles to see Logic Pro 9's default font set shown in Figure 8.8.

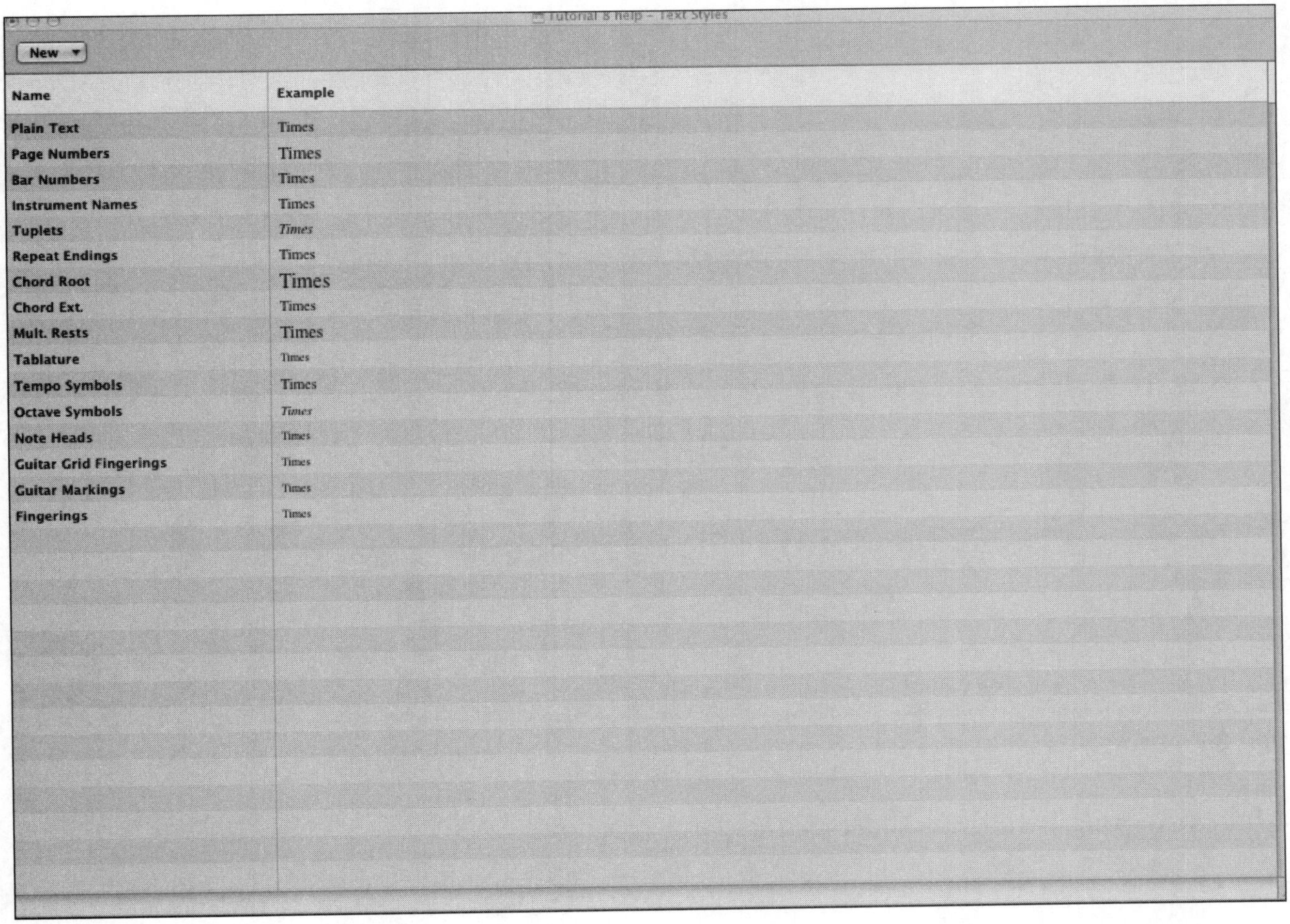

Name	Example
Plain Text	Times
Page Numbers	Times
Bar Numbers	Times
Instrument Names	Times
Tuplets	*Times*
Repeat Endings	Times
Chord Root	Times
Chord Ext.	Times
Mult. Rests	Times
Tablature	Times
Tempo Symbols	Times
Octave Symbols	*Times*
Note Heads	Times
Guitar Grid Fingerings	Times
Guitar Markings	Times
Fingerings	Times

Figure 8.8 The default text styles.

In Figure 8.9, you can see the first page of a song from a new musical by composer Claudio Merloni, who I am doing score prep for. I created some text styles for the title, composer and orchestrator, and tempos and directions. In Figure 8.10, you can see an excerpt from a film cue by film composer David Kitay. Both the orchestration and score prep are by Bill Levine. Although Bill also frequently creates text styles, in this case, he created one and relied on the Resize tool for other tasks.

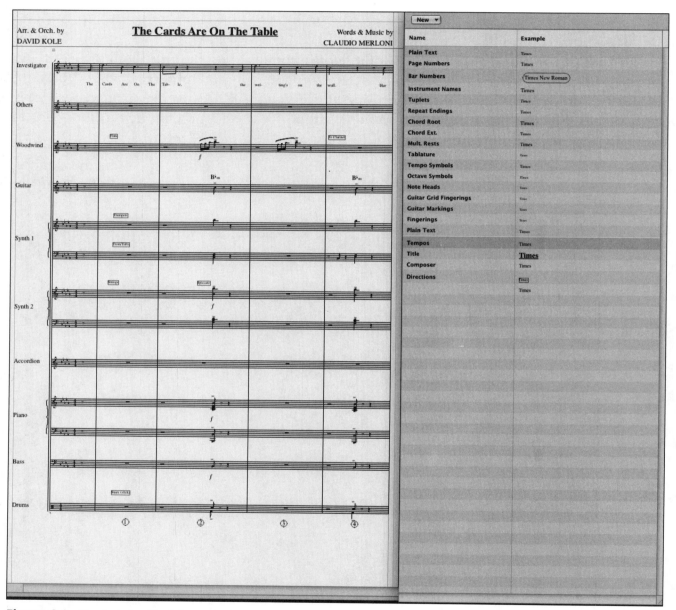

Figure 8.9 Text styles that I created.

I will be exploring both of these techniques with you now.

1. In the Text Styles menu, choose New > New Text Style. One appears in the list, cleverly named New Text Style. See Figure 8.11.

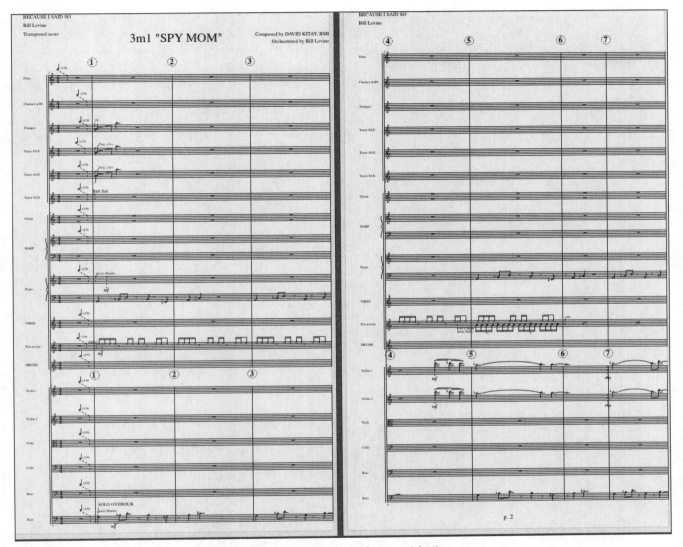

Figure 8.10 An excerpt from Bill Levine's Logic project for David Kitay.

2. Double-click the name and rename it **Directions**. Click the default Times font in the Examples column to open the Fonts window.

3. Choose a font and font size. Decide whether to have the text circled, boxed, or underlined, or any combination thereof. Stick with Times, make it size 10, and box it. The choices are reflected in the Text Style Window's Example column. See Figure 8.12.

4. Choose the text group in the Part Box. Then choose the word *Text* and drag it to insert the direction Majestically, as you see in Figure 8.13.

5. You can't see the choices you made for the Direction text style, because the Score Editor defaults to Plain Text. If you highlight it, in the Display Parameter Box you can see that Plain Text is the default. See Figure 8.14.

6. Click Plain Text and, while holding, scroll down to Directions. Now the direction appears as intended. See Figure 8.15.

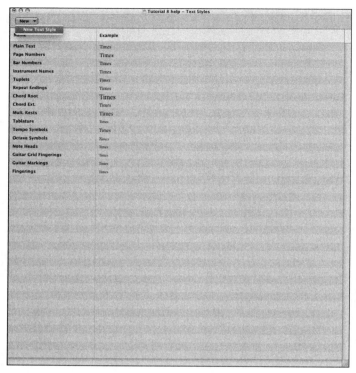

Figure 8.11 Creating a new text style.

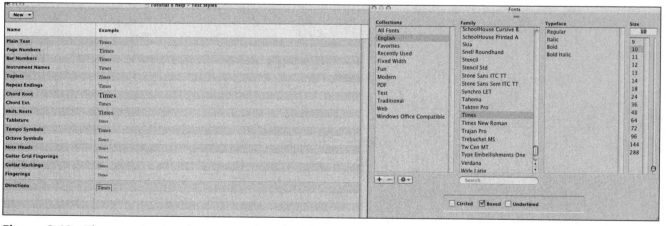

Figure 8.12 The new text style renamed and with specific font choices.

You will want to spend serious time experimenting with all the independent symbols, note extensions, and global symbols that Logic Pro provides. It is an impressive palette!

Headers and Footers

Headers and footers are the places where you insert text and symbols that have global applications. In Figure 8.16, you can see that I have switched to Page View with Print View and Show Margins checked. This allows a header and a footer area. You can resize both by adjusting their lines, but be careful—you must make sure they fall within your printer's default margins. In this case, I am leaving the sizes as is.

You will need to insert some things into the header: title, composer, orchestrator, and so on. you can use the method that I used to create text styles, but this time I demonstrate a different approach.

Figure 8.13   Entering my direction.

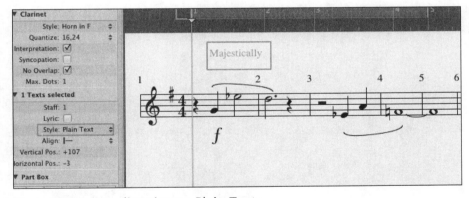

Figure 8.14   My direction as Plain Text.

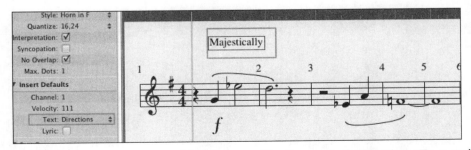

Figure 8.15   My direction with my specifically created Directions Text style.

Figure 8.16 A part in Page/Print View showing the margins.

1. Insert a title by dragging the text from the Part Box into the header at bar position 1 1 1 1. (In my experience, it is best to drag from just under the header and then up into it, keeping an eye on the help tag.) Then insert another for **Words & Music by**. It also is centered just below the title, but that is not where you want it.

2. In the Text Box (second box in the Inspector), hold the mouse down on Align and switch it to align the selected text to the right margin, as you see in Figure 8.17.

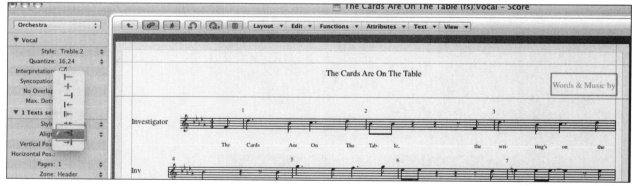

Figure 8.17 "Words & Music by" aligned to the right margin.

3. In the same manner, I now add the composer's name and align it to the right margin. "Orch. by" and the orchestrator's name are aligned to the left margin. I move their positions so that they are vertically aligned to the same number I see in the text box. See Figure 8.18.

4. I move their positions so they are vertically aligned to the same number I see in the text box, as shown in Figure 8.18.

Figure 8.18 Aligned text entries in the header.

Note   You can also use the Resize tool to create new text styles. Press Esc and choose the font. Hold the mouse down on the title and scale objects to +4.

---

5.   Shift-select the composer and orchestrator credit text. Scale objects to -2. Press the Esc key and choose the Layout tool.

6.   Use the Layout tool to tweak the horizontal position of "Orch. by" and "Words & Music by" until they look like what you see in Figure 8.19

     In Figure 8.20, I Shift-selected the other four header entries. In the highlighted area, you can see that they are assigned only to appear on the first page. Proceed to an example where you want them to appear on every page.

Figure 8.19 Text entries in the Header scaled with the Resize tool.

Figure 8.20 Text entries in the header assigned to only appear on the first page.

7.   Drag another text entry into the header and type the name of this musical: **WANNABEE WORLD.** In the text box, change the Pages setting to All. In Figure 8.21, you can see that the musical name appears on page 2 as well.

Figure 8.21 The musical's name in the header, assigned to appear on all pages.

8.   Maybe you want the name centered in the footer instead? Select WANNABEE WORLD and press the mouse down. Still pressing, change Zone to Footer. Change the alignment to center. See Figure 8.22.

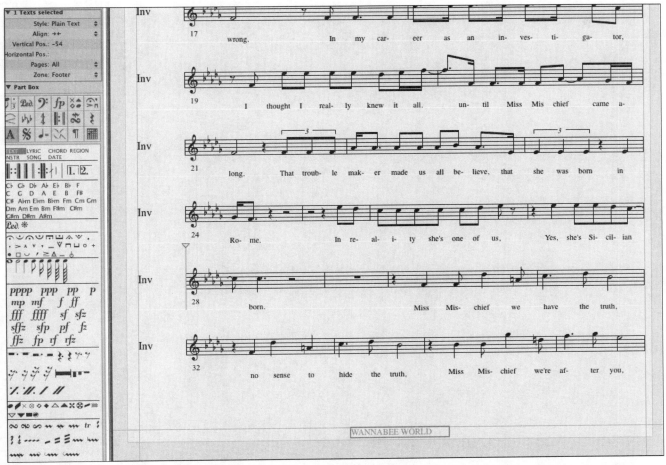

Figure 8.22   The musical's name in the footer, centered and assigned to appear on all pages.

9 Working with Cross-Staff Beaming, Doubling Instruments, and Polytonal Scores

Cross-Staff Beaming

Cross-staff beaming in the Score Editor at first seems problematic but turns out simple. On the one hand, only notes that are assigned to the same voice in a staff style can be beamed together. However, if they are assigned to the same voice, they are displayed in the same staff. In Figure 9.1, you can see I have played in a little piano part assigned to the default Piano staff style. The first two measures should be displayed with cross-staff beaming, while the remainder of the part should not be. This is another case where the Polyphonic staff style is your friend.

1. Split the region at bar 3 and assign both regions to the Piano 1/3 staff style. Fixing the second region is easy. Use the Voice Separation tool to make the top notes in the left hand change to MIDI channel 1. Now they are displayed in the top staff. See Figure 9.2.

2. That is not going to work for the first region, because you want cross-staff beaming without rests. Select the first region and duplicate the Piano 1/3 staff style. To avoid confusion, rename it **Cross Staff**. In the Voice setting for Rest, choose Hide for both voices. The result is Figure 9.3 and the regions appear as you see in Figure 9.4.

3. Rubber-band over (or Shift-select) the notes you want in the lower staff; navigate to Attributes > Voice/Staff Assignment > Staff Below Voice, as shown in Figure 9.5.

   From there you would choose the two regions and create a score set for them to have better layout control when you want to print it. Figure 9.6 shows the score set in Page View.

Doubling Instruments

It is not at all uncommon for composers and songwriters to hire a woodwind player to play more than one instrument in a song or cue; and if the instrumentalist is switching within from a C instrument, like a flute, to perhaps a Bb clarinet, you need to deal with that in the score. Now if you are like me, you keep separate Logic Pro projects for MIDI and score prep. Then the simplest method is to grab the notes played on the Bb instrument and transpose them up a whole step. There is another way.

Figure 9.1 A piano part displayed with the default Piano staff style.

Figure 9.2 The corrected display of the second region after using the Voice Separation tool.

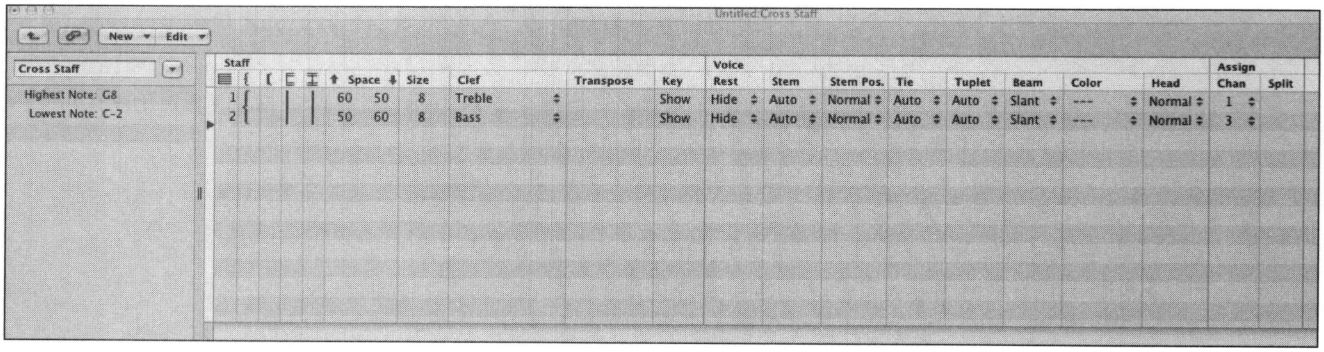

Figure 9.3 Settings in the Cross Staff staff style.

Figure 9.4 The regions with the first region set to the Cross Staff staff style.

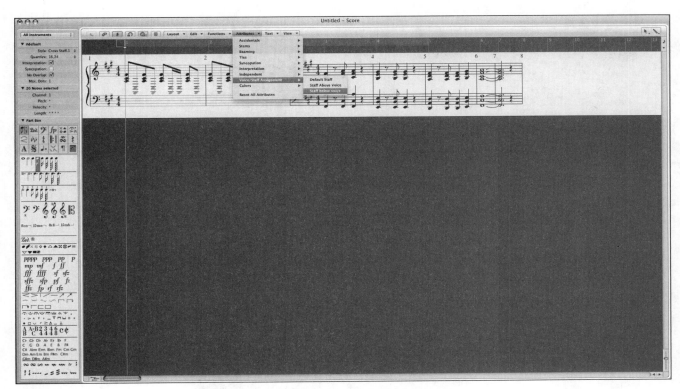

Figure 9.5   Choosing a Voice/Staff assignment for the selected notes.

Figure 9.6   A score set in Page View: first region assigned to Cross Staff staff style; second region assigned Piano 1/3 staff style.

In Figure 9.7 you can see two regions: the first assigned to the Treble staff style and the second assigned to Trumpet in Bb staff style, which is also what the clarinet needs. The score set is the default (All Instruments) and the Same Level Link (violet) is engaged. I have inserted some text to alert the player to which instrument he needs.

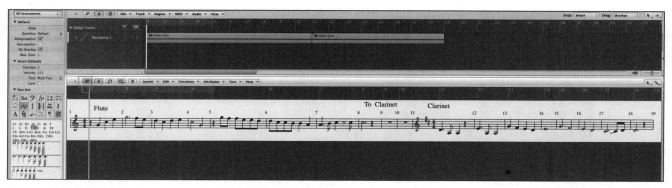

Figure 9.7 The two regions set to different staff styles.

1. What I need to do now is select the two regions. Under the Layout menu, choose Create Score Set From Selection, and it creates a score set named *Flute. Double-click and rename it **Woodwind 1**. In Page View, it looks like Figure 9.8.

Figure 9.8 The Woodwind 1 score set created for the part with two different staff styles.

2. There is, however, one remaining issue. If you choose another track and then return to this score set with the (yellow) Content Link (which you use to print parts rather than scores), you only see the first region. See Figure 9.9.

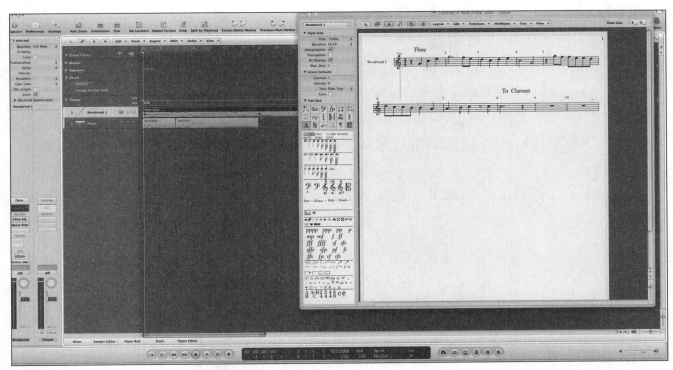

Figure 9.9 Only the first region is displayed when returning to the track with Content Link engaged.

3. Select the two regions in the Arrange area. Under the Region menu, select Folder > Pack Folder. See Figure 9.10. As you can see in Figure 9.11, even in Content Link, you can see the entire woodwind part.

Figure 9.10 Packing the two regions into a folder.

Figure 9.11 The Woodwind 1 part correctly displayed in Content Link.

Polytonal Scores

It is not exactly avant garde to write a film cue that is simultaneously in two keys. The method has been in concert hall music for over 100 years, and nearly as long in film music. Someone, however, forgot to tell the Logic Pro developers, as key signatures are global in Logic Pro. So if I want the notes to be displayed in the Score Editor in different keys, I can trick Logic Pro into doing this, in part, by using the transposing function of staff styles to alter the displayed key signatures of individual regions, but then the notes do not display really correctly. Is there a way to trick it in Logic Pro? Yes, and it is a very clever one including a transformer, meta events, and user rests. Johannes Prischl diligently explains this in his 1996 book *The Logic Notation Guide*.

I would rather undergo dental torture such as that depicted in the film *Marathon Man*. If you follow my suggestion and keep separate projects for MIDI sound and score printout, accomplishing this is a no brainer. In Figure 9.12 I have written a short example where clearly the flute and oboe are in Eb, while the clarinet and bassoon are in C. That is how I want them displayed, and I want the key signatures of each part to reflect this.

Figure 9.12   A polytonal piece of music at concert pitch.

1.   Assign Flute to Treble staff style. Duplicate and open it.

2.   Double-click the name and rename it **Treble in Eb.** Double-click in the Transposition menu and type in **+3.** As you can see in Figure 9.13, the key signature of Eb shows. Unfortunately, the notes are displayed a minor 3rd higher, which will not do.

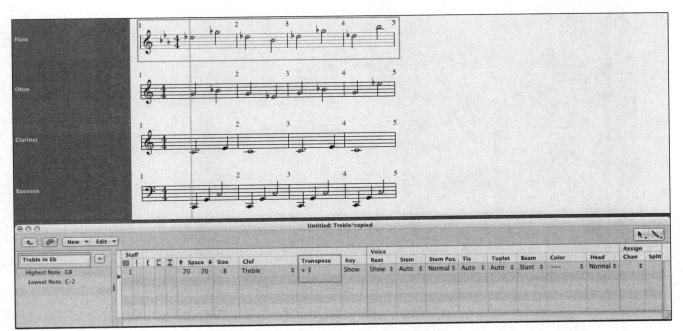

Figure 9.13   The flute in the key of Eb but notes are a minor 3rd too high.

3.   In the Arrange Window, select the Flute region. In the Region Parameter Box's Transposition field, choose –3. Now it appears as it should in the Score Editor. See Figure 9.14.

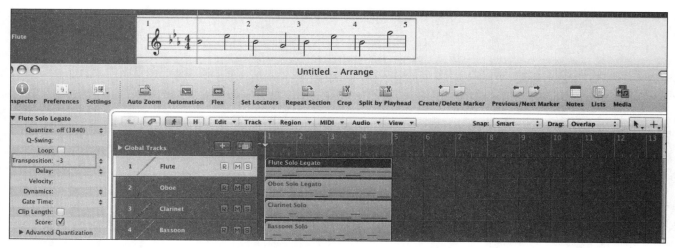

Figure 9.14 The flute in the key of Eb and notes correctly displayed.

4. Repeat the process for the oboe.

5. Because the clarinet is a Bb instrument, assign it Trumpet in Bb staff style. Now, in Figure 9.15, you can see the polytonal piece properly displayed. The bassoon part needs no modification, as it is a non-transposing instrument.

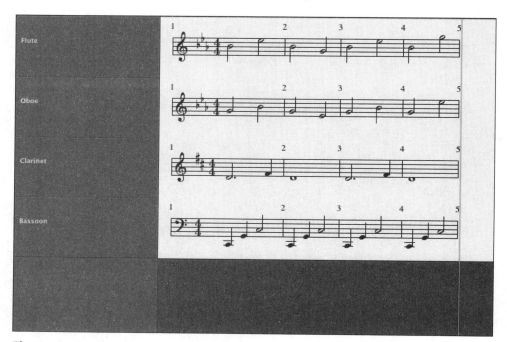

Figure 9.15 A polytonal piece properly displayed.

6. Press Play. It all sounds in the key of C—not polytonal.

7. The Track Parameter Box is below the Display Parameter Box in the Arrange Window's Inspector. The Track Parameter Box affects the software instrument, not just the region. Set Transposition to +3 for Flute and then Oboe. See Figure 9.16. Now it looks and sounds polytonal.

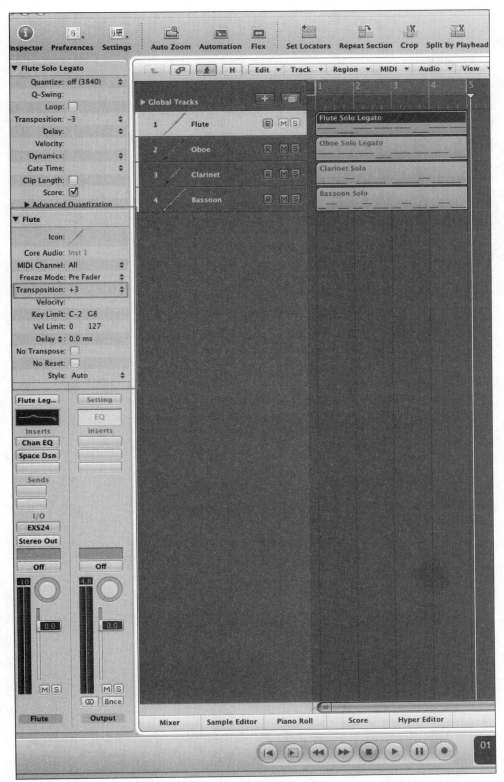

Figure 9.16 Transposing the actual pitch of the software instrument in the Track Parameter Box.

10 Working with Time Signatures

Time Signatures and Beaming

In Tutorial 7, I demonstrate how to unbeam notes by using equal subpositions. This methodology is powerful and flexible, but sometimes down and dirty is enough. How notes are beamed by default is related to the time signature (or meter, as it is also known). Figure 10.1 shows a solo part in 4/4; the Score Editor defaulted to grouping the 8th notes by four, but you want them in groups of two.

1. Double-click directly on the 4/4 time signature to open the Time Signature Window. In the Beat Grouping field, type **1+1+1+1** to tell the Score Editor to group them by quarter notes; see Figure 10.2. The result is shown in Figure 10.3.

2. Drag in the 3/4 time signature, it defaults to groups of two. If you want them to be in groups of four, double-click and type **2+2+2+2** in the Beat Grouping field. Fine and dandy. See Figure 10.4.

    This mostly works well, but see the triplet-based melody in Figure 10.5? It was played in 4/4 even though you really want to display it as 12/8—perhaps my biggest, most long-standing complaint about Logic Pro is its inability to beat dotted quarter notes in 12/8 and 6/8. Hearing the click beat 8th notes at a fast tempo is incredibly distracting! No problem. You can simply change the time signature to 12/8.

3. There is no 12/8 symbol in the Part Box, but there is an A/B symbol, which I drag in at bar 1. Upon doing so, the Time Signature Window opens again, and I define it as 12/8, as you can see in Figure 10.6.

4. But now it looks like what you see in Figure 10.7, which is incorrect. You need another method.

Converting from 4/4 Triplets to 12/8

The first thing you need to do is make sure that the region is the correct length for 12/8. This can be accomplished by time-compressing the MIDI regions. In Figure 10.8, you can see its length in the Event List, which is well over two bars (when in 12/8 it should be exactly two bars long).

Figure 10.1 The 8th notes in 4/4 with the default beaming.

Figure 10.2 Beat grouping in the Time Signature Window.

Figure 10.3 The 8th notes in 4/4 beamed in groups of two.

Figure 10.4 The 8th notes in 3/4 beamed in groups of four.

Figure 10.5 The triplet-based melody in 4/4.

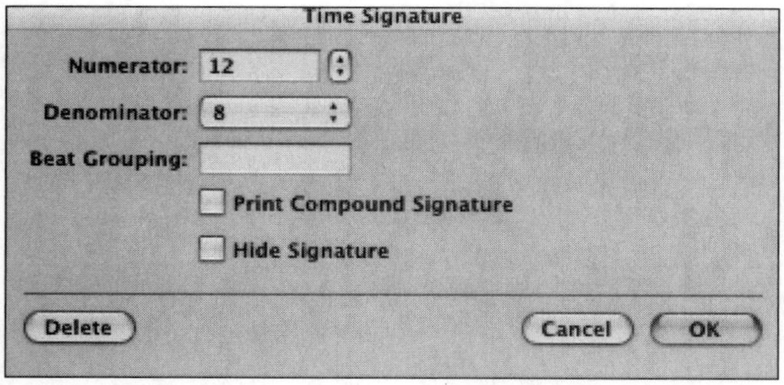

Figure 10.6   Defining the A/B time signature as 12/8.

Figure 10.7   The solo part incorrectly displayed in 12/8.

Figure 10.8   The region is too long.

1. Double-click, type **2**, and press Return. Now it is exactly two bars, as you can see in Figure 10.9. But the display still does not look correct. Oh, dear!

Figure 10.9   The region is the right length but remains incorrect.

2. Press Command-Z to undo the region length change. Navigate to the Arrange area. While holding the Option key, grab the lower-right corner; keeping an eye on the help tag, compress the region. (Logic Pro says Stretch, but it is negative stretching or compressing.) See Figure 10.10. Now in Figure 10.11, it finally looks correct.

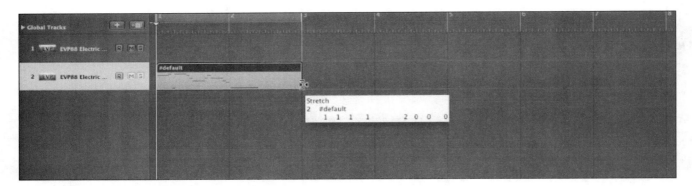

Figure 10.10   Compressing the region.

Figure 10.11   The region in 12/8 is now correct.

Compound Time Signatures

Compounding time signatures is very easy and similar to the beat grouping you did earlier. Figure 10.12 shows a similar part in 5/8, but you want to see it displayed as a 3+2 compound time signature.

Figure 10.12   The solo part in 5/8.

1. Double-click the 5/8 symbol to open the Time Signature Window. As you can see in Figure 10.13, Beat Grouping is 3+2. You have the option of printing the compound time signature.

    2+3 is a little bit more difficult. Notice in Figure 10.14 that the last three 8th notes in each measure are not beamed together.

Figure 10.13   The solo part displayed with a 3+2/8 compound time signature.

Figure 10.14   The solo part displayed with a 2+3/8 compound time signature, improperly beamed.

2. Individually choose each group of three and choose Beaming > Beam Selected. You can see the method in Figure 10.15. In Figure 10.16, you can see the desired result.

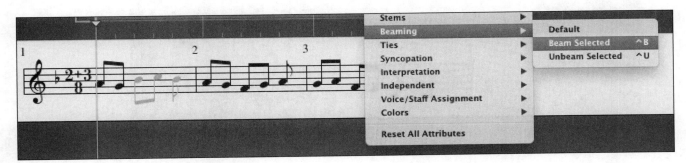

Figure 10.15   Beaming selected notes.

Figure 10.16 The solo part displayed with a 2+3/8 compound time signature, beamed correctly.

Hiding Time Signatures

Hiding time signatures can be useful for compositions that have a great number of bars of different lengths, cadenzas, and the like. Here, you go back to using a simple *5/8* time signature.

1. Double-click the *5/8* symbol to open the Time Signature Window. As you can see in Figure 10.17, the time signature is hidden. It looks funny, but surely if you switch to Page View > Print View, it will look fine. Err. . .no. See Figure 10.18.

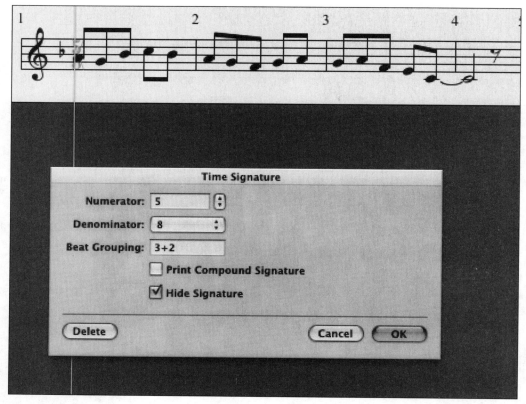

Figure 10.17 Hiding the time signature looks funny in Linear View.

Figure 10.18   Hiding the time signature looks funny in Print View.

Figure 10.19   The time signature is hidden in Print Preview.

2.   The truth is that it will print fine. Press Command-P and choose Preview. There you can see that it will print without the time signature displayed. See Figure 10.19.

11 Editing and Copying Options in the Score Editor

Changing Note Length with Duration Bars and Sustain Pedal to Note Length

It is not exactly a secret among long-time Logic Pro users that very few Score Editor improvements have been forthcoming. However, Logic Pro 9 has a feature for altering the length of multiple notes without ever leaving the Score Editor or opening another editor (called Duration Bars). Figure 11.1 shows the View menu's Duration Bars option. Here, the Selected Notes option is enabled.

1. Shift-select several notes that you want to make longer. You can see the Duration Bar handles. See Figure 11.2.

2. Drag the notes to the length you would like them; keep an eye on the help tag. See Figure 11.3. In Figure 11.4, you can see that the notes are lengthened.

   A nice feature is the ability to convert pedaling, which is MIDI controller 64, to note length. Figure 11.5 shows a series of quarter notes that sound like whole notes because the sustain pedal continues the sound. You can eliminate the pedaling but convert the notes to their proper display as whole notes.

3. Under the Functions menu, choose Note Events > Sustain Pedal to Note Length, as shown in Figure 11.6. They are converted to whole notes and the pedals are gone. See Figure 11.7.

Copying within the Same Region

There are a number of ways to accomplish the task of copying within a region in the Score Editor. In Figure 11.8, you can see a string quintet with notes, attachments, and dynamics entered only in the Violin 1 part. You will copy what you see entered into that same region. Most users would select the events and, while holding the Option key, drag them to the desired location and transpose (i.e., a half step up), if desired, and of course that works perfectly well. But perhaps the most direct way (if you hate mousing around, as I do) is to use Copy MIDI Events, under the Functions menu. I use this so often that I have assigned a single keystroke to it—F13—as you can see in Figure 11.9.

93

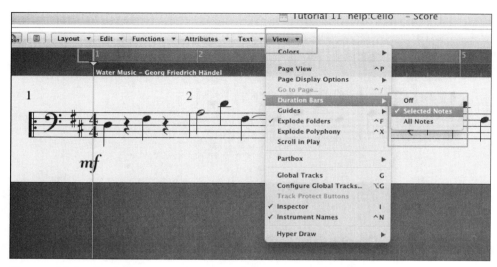

Figure 11.1 Enabling Duration Bars for Selected Notes.

Figure 11.2 Duration Bars handles are now visible.

Figure 11.3 Lengthening multiple notes with Duration Bars.

Figure 11.4   The notes after lengthening with Duration Bars.

Figure 11.5   A part with quarter notes and sustain pedals.

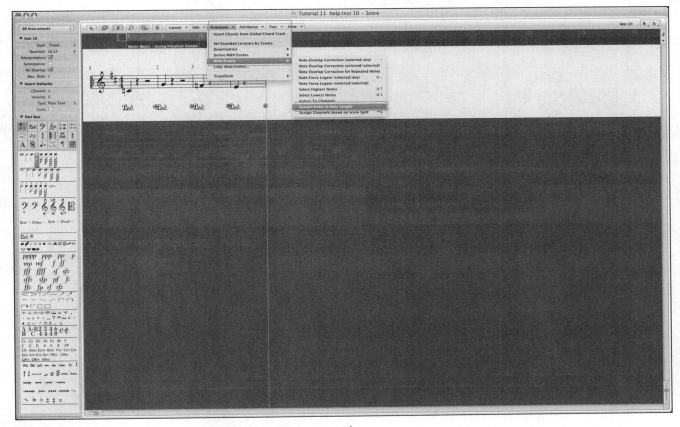

Figure 11.6   Converting Sustain Pedals to Note Length.

Figure 11.7   The part is now converted to whole notes with no sustain pedals.

Figure 11.8 The string quintet with notes, attachments, and dynamics in the first violin staff.

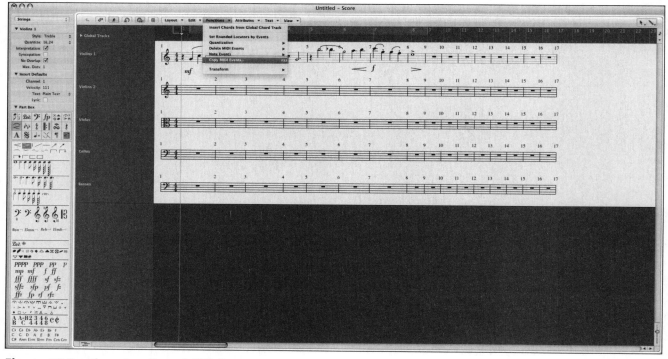

Figure 11.9 Choosing Copy MIDI Events.

1. Under the Functions menu, choose Copy MIDI Events (or assign and press a keyboard shortcut like F13). The Copy MIDI Events Window opens. The default is Copy Merge, though you have a number of choices. See Figure 11.10. In this case, Copy Merge is what you want.

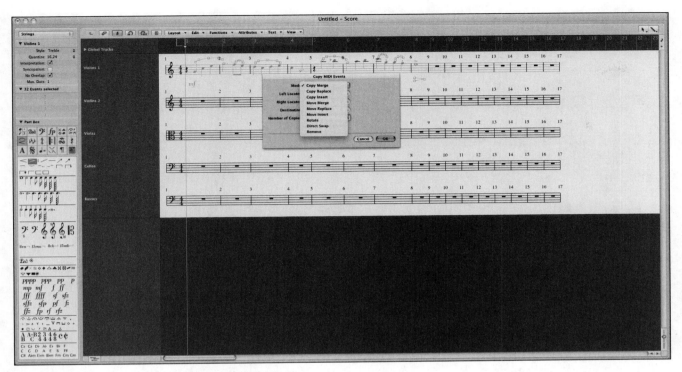

Figure 11.10 The Copy MIDI Events Window.

2. Now make absolutely certain of the first event position you want to copy. If you have
    hard quantized this (it is for score printout only), you do not care if it sounds rigid; the
    event is at the second beat of bar 1 and ends after bar 8. Type **1 2 1 1** in the Left Locator
    field, type **9 1 1 1** in the Right Locator field, and type **9 1 1 1** in the Destination field.
    Leave Number of Copies at 1 and leave Create New Region unchecked. See Figure 11.11.

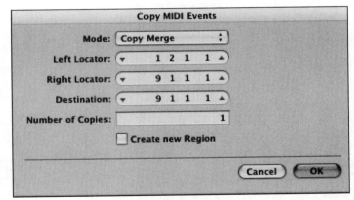

Figure 11.11 Entering choices in the Copy MIDI Events fields.

3. Click OK to copy. However, you want this transposed up a half tone. Here is where key
    commands are your friend. With the events selected, press the default key command for
    Event Transpose +1. (In the U.S., the numeric keyboard preset is Option-up arrow.) See
    Figure 11.12.

Figure 11.12 The events have been copied to bar 9, transposed up a half tone.

Note It is worth noting that while the function is called Copy MIDI Events, many of the score symbols are treated by Logic Pro as MIDI events and will be copied as well.

4. The Cello part in Figure 11.13 has a motif that you want to repeat. Rubber-band over the notes so all are selected. Press Command-R for Repeat Regions/Events; its window opens. For Number of Copies, type **29**. Leave Adjustment at Auto. See Figure 11.14.

Figure 11.13 The cello motif.

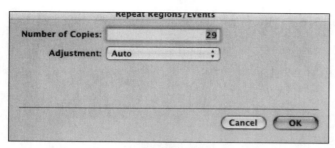

Figure 11.14 Setting in the Repeat Regions/Events Window.

5. Wait. You need the notes from bar 9 on to be transposed up a half tone. Select the first C in bar 9 and press Shift-F. This command is for Select All Following (under the Edit menu). See Figure 11.15.

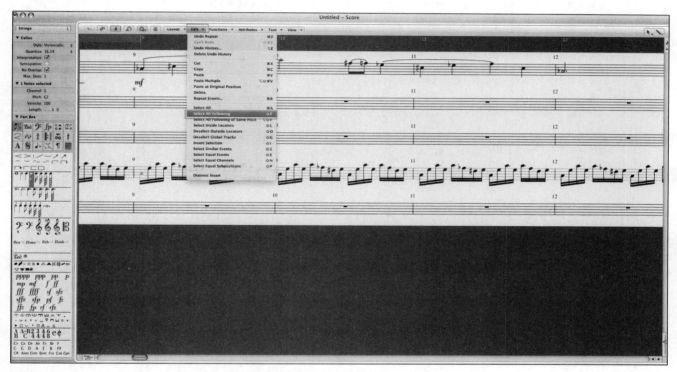

Figure 11.15 Select All Following under the Edit menu.

6. Press Option-up arrow to Event Transpose +1.

You can repeat whole measures and regions in this fashion as well. The important thing is to check your quantization. You may think you are copying from a particular bar, but if events are at (for example) 8 4 4 239, they will not be included.

Copying to Other Regions at the Same Bar Position

One feature I have requested for a long time is the ability to copy via Option-dragging notes and symbols from one region into another. That request has not been implemented, so we must use other methods. Copying from one region to another at the same bar position is pretty easy and fast. In this case, you want to copy the Violin 1 events simultaneously to the Violin 2 and Viola regions.

1. Select the first event (mezzo-forte symbol) in the Violin 1 region. Press Shift-F for Select All Following.

2. Press Command-C to copy the selected events to the clipboard. Select the Violin 2 and Viola regions. In Figure 11.16, you can see that the playhead is not a bar 1, even though that is where you will want to paste the events. Why? Because you will use the key command Paste Multiple at Original Position. That key command is not assigned. By default there is a key command for plain ol' Paste Multiple, so you could move the playhead to the proper position—but that is too much work.

Figure 11.16 The Violin 1 events are copied and the other two regions are selected but not at the intended paste position in the playhead.

3. Assign the key command to Option-Shift-Command-P. See Figure 11.17. (Obviously you will have to realign slurs in the Viola part.)

Figure 11.17 The Violin 1 events are pasted into the other two regions using the Paste Multiple at Original Position key command.

4. Copy the first note of the cello motif on beats 1and 3 into the Bass region. Shift-select the two notes; under the Edit menu, choose Select Equal Events. See Figure 11.18.

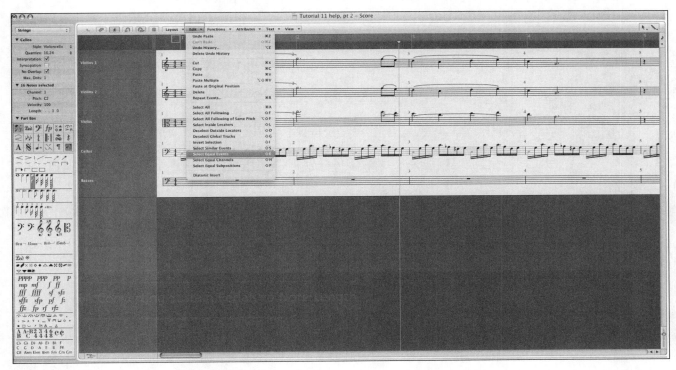

Figure 11.18 Select Equal Events.

5. Press Command-C, select the Bass region, and then press Option-Shift-Command-P. In Figure 11.19, you can see how well it has worked.

Figure 11.19 The cello notes pasted into the Bass region.

Copying to Other Regions at a Different Bar Position

Copying to other regions at a different bar position is simple and only requires the additional step of placing the playhead at the proper position in the project.

1. Select the first event (mezzo-forte symbol) in the Violin 1 region. Press Shift-F to select all.

2. Press Command-C to copy them to the clipboard; select the Violin 2 and Viola regions. In Figure 11.20, you can see that Go To Position Window, accessed by key command, will advance the playhead to where you want to copy the Violin 1 events.

Figure 11.20 Using the Go To Position key command to advance the playhead.

3. Press Option-Shift-Command-V. See Figure 11.21.

Figure 11.21 The Violin 1 events pasted into the other two regions at a different bar position using Paste Multiple.

12 Creating Drum Notation from GM and non-GM Drum Kits

The following holds true in a General MIDI drum kit:

- B0 and C1 are kick drums
- C#1 is a sidestick
- D1–E1 are snares
- F1, A1, C2, and D2 are toms; F#1 is a closed hi-hat, and so on.

Drum kits programmed using these conventions make it easy to play through a variety of different General MIDI kits without having to hunt and peck for keys that trigger specific drum sounds. While no two GM drum kits are precisely alike, all have the basic kit pieces assigned to the same notes. But for the purposes of creating standard drum notation, those notes are all wrong! You're more likely to see the note A1 indicating the kick drum on a drum chart than the GM notes used to play kicks (B0 and C1).

However, in more deeply sampled or non-GM drum kits—like those found in BFD2, Superior Drummer, and XLN's Addictive Drums—there may well be more kicks and more snares. Hence, the mapping can be quite different. This tutorial uses XLN's Addictive Drums.

To translate the notes used to trigger sounds into those you need displayed in a drum part, you will use the #Drums staff style—a special type of staff style that uses a behind-the-scenes process called the *mapped instrument. Mapping* means taking a MIDI note (like C1) and telling the Score Editor to display it as if it were another note (in the case of the kick drum, A1). Similarly, the mapped instrument takes the F#1, G#1, and A#1 used to play GM hi-hats and maps them to appear above the top line of the staff (B2). It can make a note head appear as a (circled) X.

If you truly want to preserve the sound of your drum parts while changing only the notes displayed on the score, you can access additional mapped instrument features by creating another mapped instrument in the environment. Aside from displaying the appropriate notes for drum notation, this powerful environment object lets you name notes and assign one or more sounds to one note (or vice versa). However, while using it is simple, using the mapped drum in a staff style and making it properly reflect the way you want it to look is time-consuming. It is so time-consuming that even the fearless Johannes Prischl, author of the *Logic Notation Guide*, suggested that you might want to keep two versions of the part: one for sound and one for display.

Since that is my approach, this tutorial deals with that scenario. You will use the #Drums staff style and take advantage of its pre-programmed capabilities for mapping the notes you played to the notes you want to see in the score.

To give you some insight about how this all works, see Figure 12.1. I have created a mapped instrument in the environment and opened it by double-clicking it. Since it pertains to more than drums, I cannot fit the whole display into one picture, so I am choosing the notes that pertain to the important drum kit pieces. This briefly explains why things look as they do when you switch to the default #Drums staff style later in this tutorial.

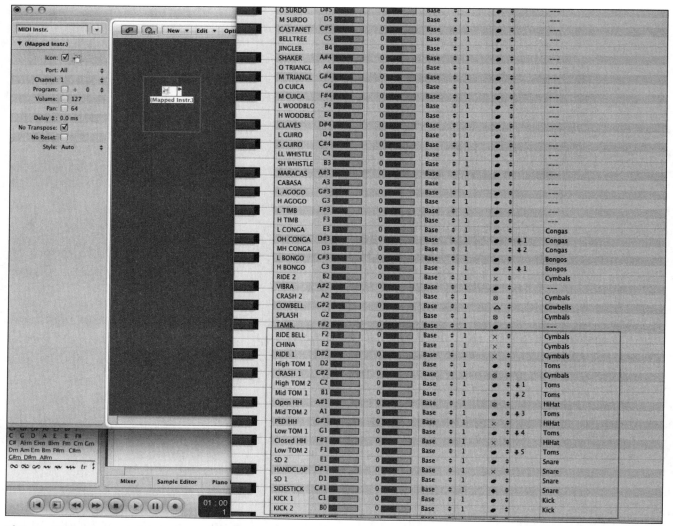

Figure 12.1 Notes in the mapped instrument and their display choices.

The default mapped instrument is pre-programmed to re-map the display of 28 specific notes. That could be inadequate for a complex part that cannot realistically be played by a single drummer. Because you are striving for a part that is actually readable and playable by a real drummer, this is just fine. And getting your recorded notes to conform to these preset note mappings is simply a matter of transposing the notes in the MIDI region to these 28 notes.

In Figure 12.2, you can see a part performed with a non-GM drum kit in Bass Clef. I used a snare assigned to C#1 in the first four bars and switch to another, assigned to E1, in the next four measures. In the first four bars, I am playing two hi-hats, one assigned to C#2 and the other to D#2. A toms fill is in bar 4, and at bar 5, the ride cymbal takes over from the hi-hats. Then the staff style changes to the default #Drums and it appears as you see in Figure 12.3. While this is clear and readable, it does not follow the long-established staff position of note assignments used for drum notation in the U.S. Choosing the #Drums staff style and changing some settings is insufficient.

Figure 12.2 A drum part played with a non-GM drum kit displayed in the Bass staff style.

Figure 12.3 The drum part played with a non-GM drum kit displayed in the default #Drums staff style.

While all the MIDI editors could be utilized for what you do next, you will use a Piano Roll and the Event List for this task.

1. In the Piano Roll, press Shift and click the C#1 key and the E1 key. The notes played on both snare sounds are selected, as you can see in Figure 12.4.

2. Hold down Shift-Option in the Event List and grab one of the snare notes, then drag it up to D1. See Figure 12.5.

3. Repeat the process for the closed hi-hats, Shift-selecting the C#2 and D#2 notes and changing them to F#1.

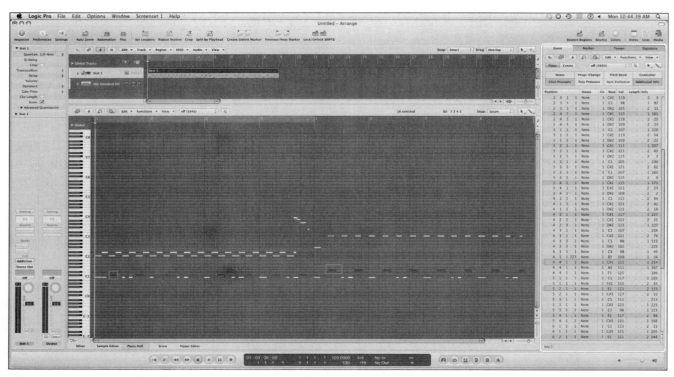

Figure 12.4 Selecting all the snare notes.

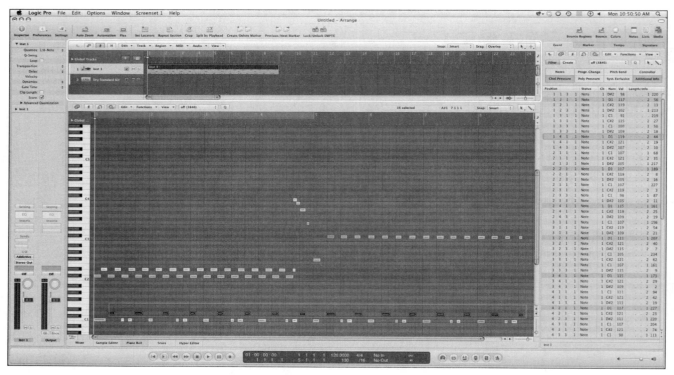

Figure 12.5 All the snare hits now assigned to D1.

4. Rubberband select the toms in the fill, which were played on C4, B3, A3, and F3. *Without* holding any modifier keys, drag the C4 down to D2. The others change respectively. This puts them in the range of the GM standard for toms. See Figure 12.6.

5. Select the ride cymbal notes on C#3 and drag them to D#2, the GM default for ride cymbal. In Figure 12.7, you can see that they appear in the Bass staff style, and in Figure 12.8 they appear in the #Drums staff style.

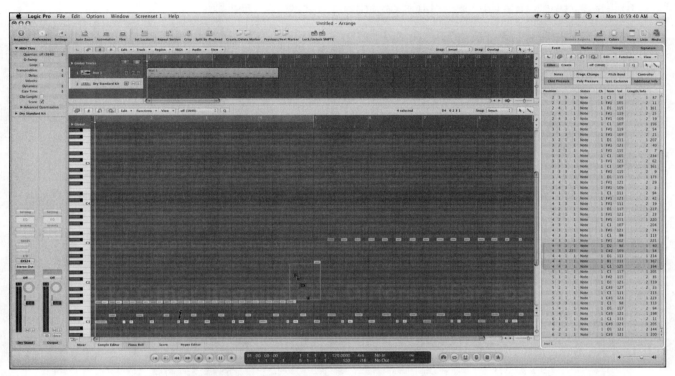

Figure 12.6 Changing the toms fill note pitches in the Event List.

Figure 12.7 All the notes as they appear in the Bass staff style.

Figure 12.8 All the notes as they appear in the #Drums staff style.

We are in the ballpark but the part still does not look right by U.S. conventions. You can correct this by adjusting some of the various #Drums staff style parameters. But rather than mess with the default #Drums staff style, it is better to create a duplicate and work with that.

1. Double-click the #Drums staff style to open it. Under New, choose Duplicate Staff Style. That way, any changes you make will not affect the original. Reassign the part to the duplicated staff style and double-click to open it. The default positions for kit piece groups are in the window. See Figure 12.9. Rename the duplicated staff style **#Trap Set** for importing later into templates or other projects.

2. Change the Kick group position from down 4 to 3.5; change the snare from down 2 to 1.5. Adjust both Hi-Hat and Cymbals to down 0.5. These adjustments move the notes to display on the lines and spaces you want. If the value is set to a whole number, the group's notes will appear on a line, while with an added 0.5, it will appear on a space.

3. In the Voice column, click the line for the kick to add a voice. This allows the kick stems down with the snare stems up, as you can see in Figure 12.10.

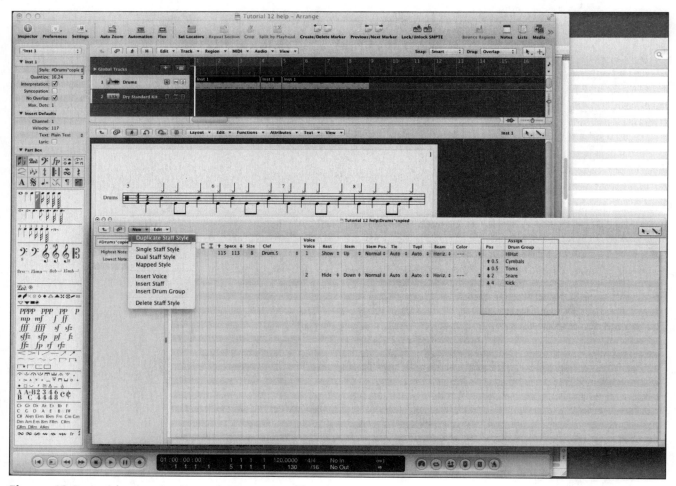

Figure 12.9 Inside the duplicated #Drums staff style.

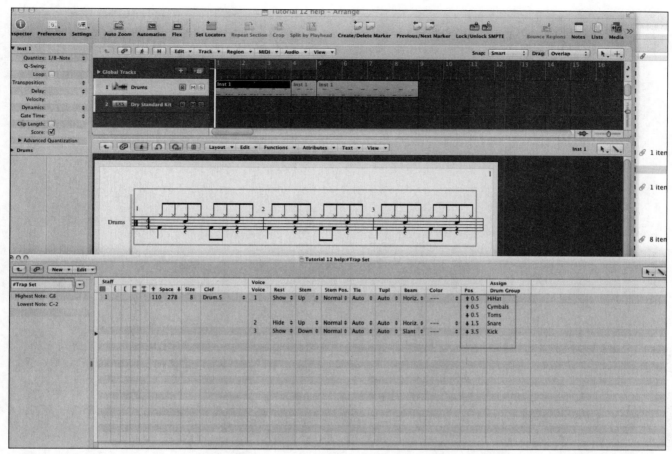

Figure 12.10 Changing the note display positions and adding a voice in the #Trap Set staff style.

Fixing the Toms Fill

In Figure 12.11, you can see the whole part. The bar with the toms fill is a hot mess!

1. Use the Marque tool to create a separate region for the fill measure.

2. Duplicate the #Trap Set staff style, rename it **#Trap Set Fill**, and assign it to the region with the toms fill.

3. Inside the staff style, under the Voice menu, click 2, and voice 2 disappears.

4. In line with the Kick drum group, click in the Voice field. Voice 2 now includes only the Kick group. Hide the rests for the second voice. See Figure 12.12.

Figure 12.11 The toms fill is not looking good.

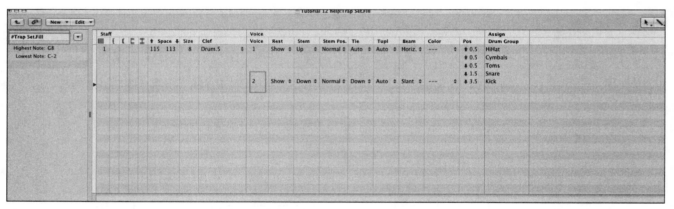

Figure 12.12 Changing voice 2 in the staff style.

5. Because this is a different fill, in the Event List, change the tom notes to those you see in Figure 12.13. Notice that I made the tom fill a little simpler for the drummer to read. Now all looks good when you choose the third region, which is assigned to the #Trap Set staff style—except this is a ride cymbal, not hi-hats. In retrospect, dragging the cymbals position with the hi-hats was not a good choice. No problem!

6. Back in the #Trap Set staff style, change the cymbals to up 2. As you can see in Figure 12.14, it looks fine. It is time to run this into one drum part.

7. Select all three regions and change Score Editor Link to Same Level Link. The whole part is now visible.

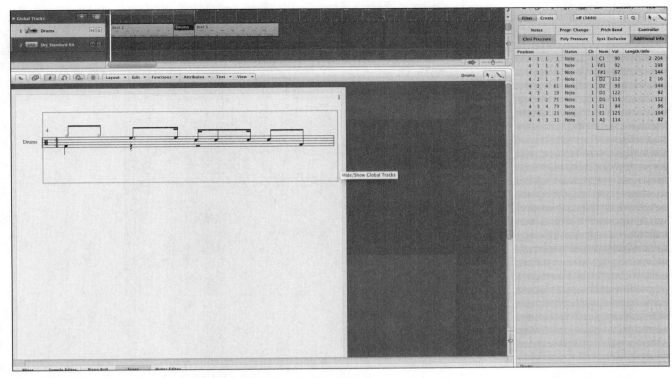

Figure 12.13   The tom fill notes adjusted for better display.

Figure 12.14   Adjusting the cymbals.

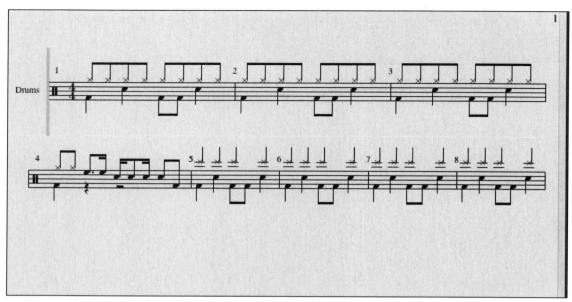

Figure 12.15 The created score set.

8.   Create a score set; see Figure 12.15.

9.   In the Rest group in the Part Box, choose the repeat symbol. Using the Pencil tool, click it into the appropriate measures.

10. With the Layout tool, drag the last measure of the first line to the second line. Add a couple of text directions and some dynamics, and voilà! See the finished trap set part in Figure 12.16.

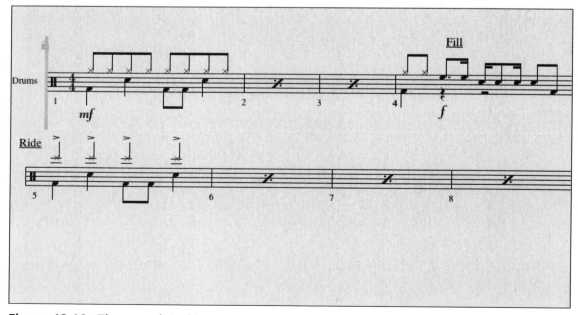

Figure 12.16 The completed trap set part.

13 Orchestral Percussion Display in the Score Editor

P ercussion is perhaps the least codified notated section of the orchestra. Firstly, the display conventions have varied quite a bit over generations, styles, and genres. However, tuned percussion instruments, like timpani and mallets, are pretty straightforward. Aside from inserting rolls into the Score Editor over rolled notes, they are not much of an issue. Figure 13.1 shows the roll symbol I inserted at bar 3. The only other thing is to defeat Interpretation on the last note and insert a user 8th rest at 4 1 3 1. (Hold the Shift key while dragging in the rest.)

I have loaded into an EXS24 a patch called Orchestral Kit that contains multiple orchestral percussion sounds—in bars 1 and 3, played in two piatti (crash cymbal) hits, and in bars 5 through 6, triangle. See Figure 13.2. Clearly, it should not look like this.

It is time to make it look more like what a percussionist needs to see when he is switching between two percussion instruments. Here is where it gets very subjective. And bear in mind that my choices are not the only acceptable choices.

1. Double-click the Bass staff style to open it.

2. Under New, choose Duplicate Staff Style. That will allow you to make modifications to the staff style that will not affect the original. See Figure 13.3.

3. Reassign the region to the duplicated staff style and double-click to open it. In the window, rename it something like Percussion 1, and in the Clef area, change the clef to Drum 1. It now appears as you see in Figure 13.4. This is a subjective choice on my part, and other drum clefs are arguably just as correct.

4. I want all the notes to be displayed just above the line, which is MIDI note B2 because this was originally in the bass clef. In the Event List, press Command-A for Select ALL, and they will all be highlighted.

5. While holding the Shift and Option keys, drag the notes in the Event List, and they will all change to the same note. Continue dragging until the notes are assigned to B2. See Figure 13.5.

6. With the piatti notes selected, go to the Part Box. The top row in the fifth group includes note heads, as you can see in Figure 13.6. Select the note head that looks like a circled X and drag it to the piatti notes in the Score Editor. See Figure 13.7.

Figure 13.1   The timpani part.

Figure 13.2   Piatti and triangle in the Bass staff style.

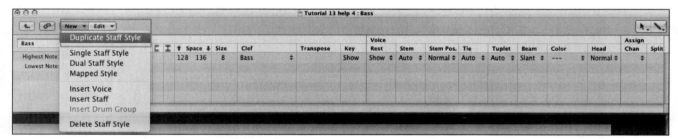

Figure 13.3   Duplicating the Bass staff style.

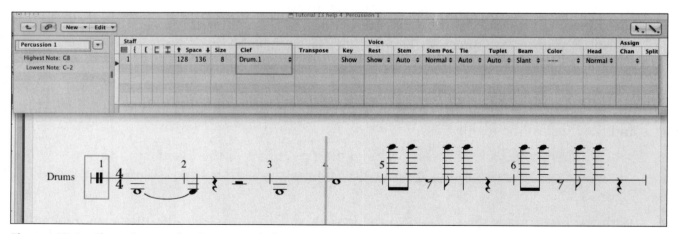

Figure 13.4   Changing to the Drum. 1 clef.

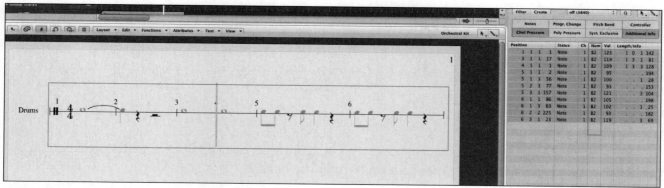

Figure 13.5   Assigning notes to B2.

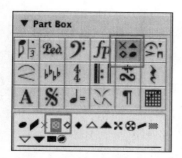

Figure 13.6   Notes in the note head group in the Part Box.

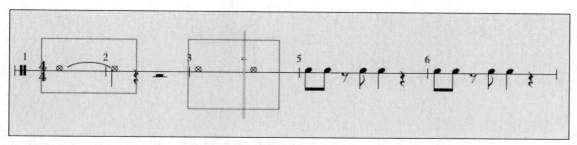

Figure 13.7   The piatti notes with the circled X note head.

7. With the triangle notes selected, return to the Part Box and select the note head that looks like a triangle. Drag it to the triangle notes in the Score Editor. They will appear as you see in Figure 13.8.

8. The stems should go up in my opinion, so in the Score Editor, press Command-A to select all the notes. Under the Attributes menu, navigate to Stems and choose Up. See Figure 13.9.

9. Add some closed and open symbols and some text. In Figure 13.10, you can see my preferred way of displaying this percussion part.

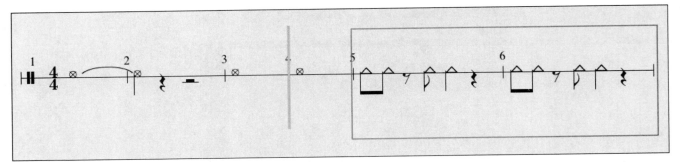

Figure 13.8 Changing the triangle notes to a preferred note head.

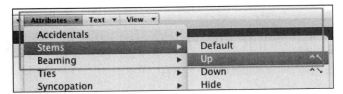

Figure 13.9 Changing the triangle notes to stems up.

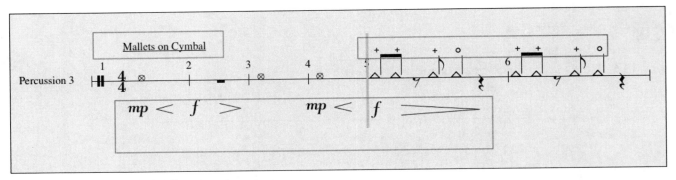

Figure 13.10 The finished percussion part.

Mallets on Cymbal Part

You will do one more: a mallets on cymbal part. This example uses that same EXS24 patch, and the mallets on cymbal part is assigned to G#1. Once again, copy the default #Drums staff style and assign it to the region. It looks like what you see in Figure 13.11, but this is not at all what you want.

1. Inside the staff style, change the clef to a single-line drum clef, as you see in Figure 13.12.

2. In the Event List (or editor of your choice), change the notes to G2. Now they are roughly where you want them to be and with the note heads you want, but they are just a little too high. See Figure 13.13.

3. Back in the staff style, change the cymbals position to up 0.5. Set Tie to Up. Figure 13.14 shows this going in the right direction.

4. Add an instrument instruction and dynamics. In Figure 13.15, you can see my end result.

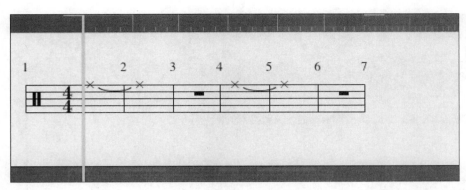

Figure 13.11   The mallets on cymbal part in the copied default #Drums staff style.

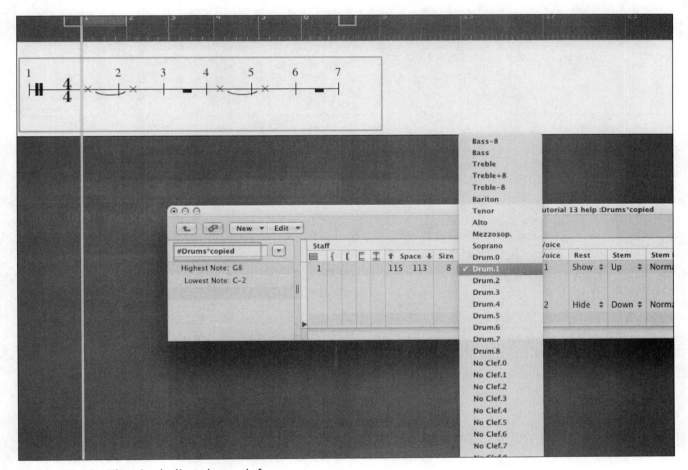

Figure 13.12   The single-line drum clef.

Once more, let me assert that a lot of my choices are subjective and may seem arbitrary. You are free to make your own choices. As long as the part is easily readable and your intentions are clear, be confident that your work is fine for a real percussionist in a recording session.

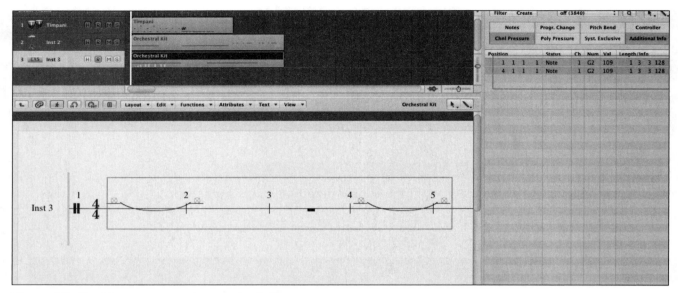

Figure 13.13   The transposed notes look better.

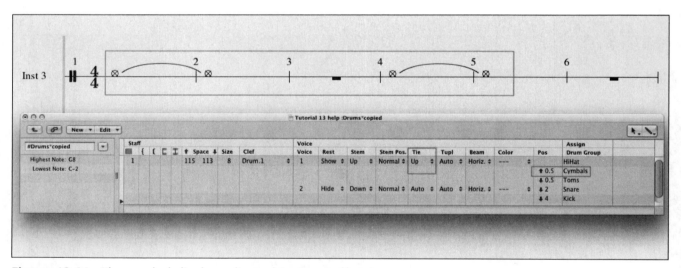

Figure 13.14   The cymbal display adjusted in the staff style.

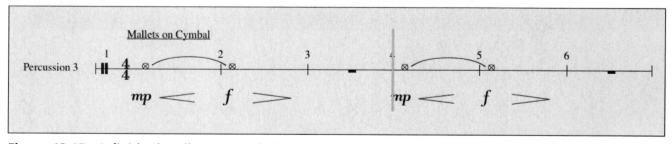

Figure 13.15   A finished mallets on cymbal part.

14 Creating Parts for Guitarists with Rhythm and Chords

Every block has half a dozen kids who play guitar. How hard can it be writing for guitar? Well, if you are writing for a classical guitarist or a virtuosic featured part in a film cue or recording, then you better spend some time with a good guitarist learning what the instrument can and cannot do well.

Rhythm

That said, most of the time most people only write melodic lines and chords and leave it to the guitarist to work through inversions and hand positions. They insert text directions like *pick* or *strum*. There are only two critical things you need to keep in mind for notation purposes:

- Guitarists want to read treble clef, not bass clef or a grand staff.

- Notes sound an octave lower than written. To hear middle C, write a note on the third space of the treble clef.

In Figure 14.1, you can see a rhythm guitar part I performed with a strummed guitar patch, in the key of A; I entered that key signature. This sounds okay with this patch, but the score as you see it here doesn't exactly represent what I want a real guitarist to play and is therefore not want he wants to see. He needs to see just the chords and the rhythm. I quantize to 8th notes—the smallest value in this case. If you have not memorized the chords you have played, make a chord sheet for later reference. Alternatively, you can duplicate the track and the region and view them both in the Score Editor, as I am doing here.

1. In bar 1, delete any notes except for one on each guitar strum, as you can see in Figure 14.2.

2. Using the same technique used in the drum tutorials, select the notes. While pressing Shift-Option, drag the notes to A3. This is strictly for how the chord slashes will look on the page and has nothing to do with the key.

3. With those notes selected, go to the Part Box and choose a large slash note head. Drag the note head onto the notes so it appears as you see in Figure 14.3. When you let go of the mouse button, it looks like what you see in Figure 14.4. The note heads of unselected

Figure 14.1   A rhythm guitar part, as played with strummed guitar patch.

Figure 14.2   One note per guitar strum.

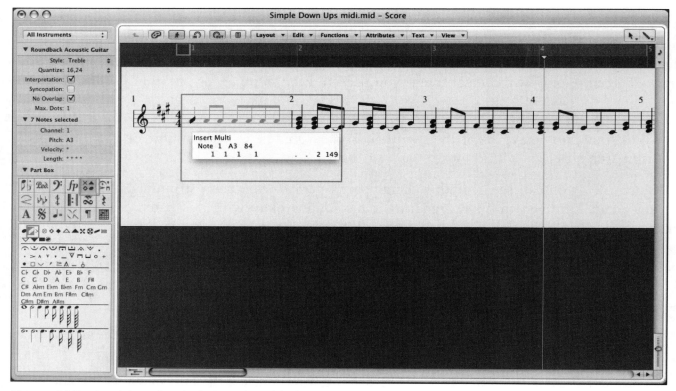

Figure 14.3   Applying the slash note head in bar 1.

notes remain unaffected. You can also do this by selecting the slash and clicking on the notes with the Pencil tool.

4.   Choose Functions > Copy MIDI Events (or use your key command). This time you are using Copy Replace to copy bar 1 to bar 2 seven times. See Figure 14.5.

Figure 14.4 The note heads changed to a slash.

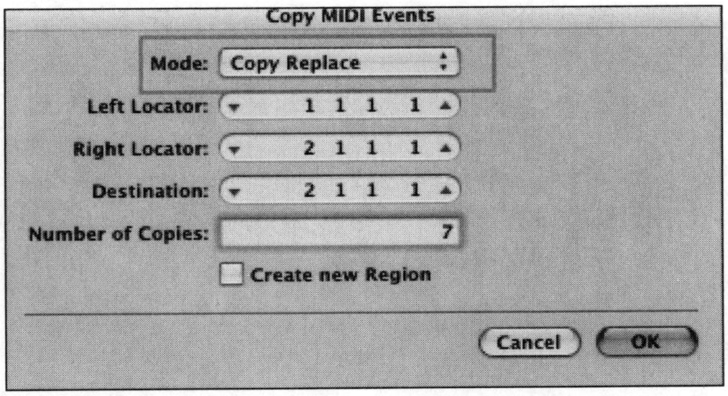

Figure 14.5 Copying and replacing bar 1 to bar 2 seven times.

Chords

When the rhythm is correct, it is time to add the chord changes.

1. In the Text group in the Part Box, choose Chord. See Figure 14.6.

2. Drag Chord over the first note, keeping an eye on the help tag to make sure it's being entered at the desired bar/beat position. See Figure 14.7. Now type the chord name.

3. Press the tab key until you reach the note where the next chord change occurs (in this case, bar 2). As you can see, chord entry is similar to lyric entry, as explained in Tutorial 8.

4. Handle the rest of the chords in a similar fashion. Press Enter or Return to end chord entry.

5. In bars 7 and 8, chords are suspended and *sus* is lower than I want; see Figure 14.8. Double-click the *B sus* to open the chord name dialog box. In Figure 14.9, you can see

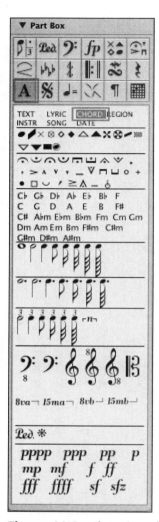

Figure 14.6 Choosing the Part Box symbol for chord entry.

sus in Root Note Extensions: Lower. It is relatively simple to press Command-X (delete) in the Lower position and Command-V (paste) in the Upper, but doing that with lots of chords would be time-consuming. An ounce of prevention is worth a pound of cure.

6. Type the Upper position and enter a comma. Subsequent typing in the entry will go to the Lower position. See Figure 14.10.

    What you now have is fine, except for some possible realigning, as you did with lyrics and text. However, since the rhythm is the same for each bar, you might choose a repeat sign and click it into bars 2–6 and bar 8 so that it appears as shown in Figure 14.11.

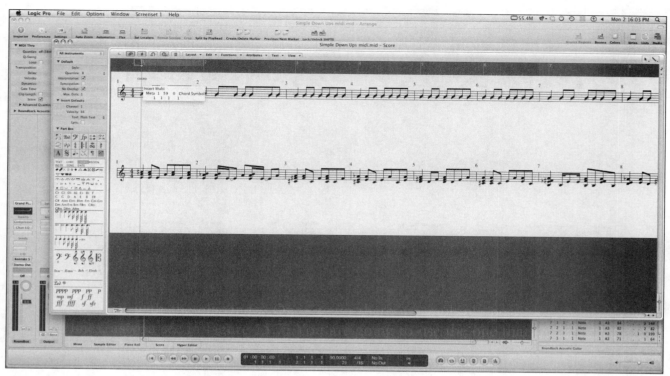

Figure 14.7   Entering a chord at bar 1.

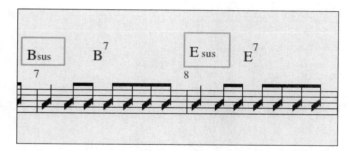

Figure 14.8   The *sus* is in a lower position.

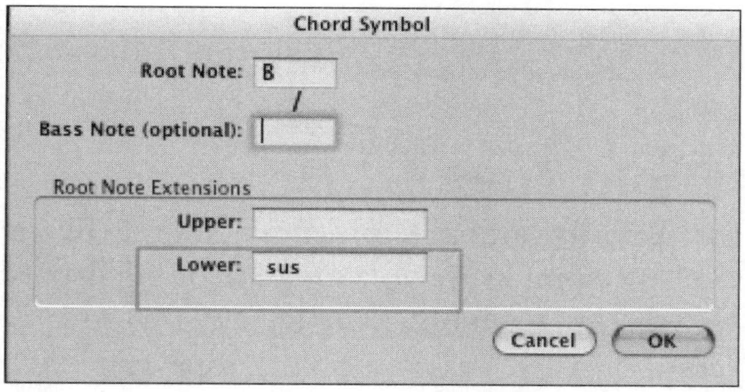

Figure 14.9   The *sus* was entered in the Lower position of the Root Note Extensions area in the Chord Symbol box.

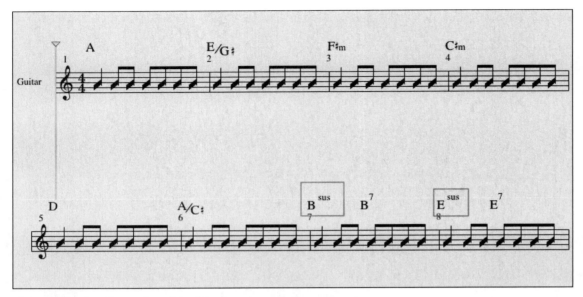

Figure 14.10 The part with the chord symbols entered.

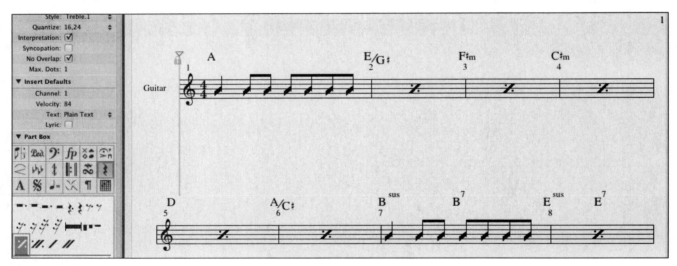

Figure 14.11 Using repeat signs for rhythmically similar bars.

Inserting Chords from the Global Chord Track

I am asked about this a lot. Though inserting chords from the global chord track sounds like a good idea, it creates more problems than it solves in my opinion. If you take an original part and, in the Global Chord track, click Analyze, you get what is shown in Figure 14.12. It is clearly not correct and has too many changes. If you composed using Apple Loops and have entered the chords manually to change them in the Global Chord track, you can then choose Insert Chords from Global Chord Track from the Functions menu. It works well if the chords are quite simple, but my advice is to avoid that method. See Figure 14.13.

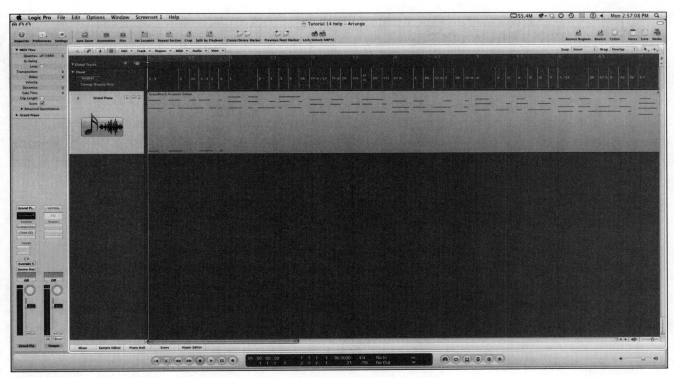

Figure 14.12   Chord analysis performed by the Global Chord track.

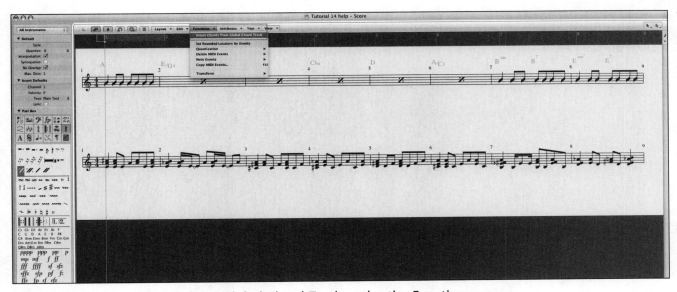

Figure 14.13   Insert Chords from Global Chord Track under the Functions menu.

Guitar Tablature and the Chord Grid

The Score Editor does indeed have the capability to create tablature with extensive choices in size, chords, and even an editor to define chords. In Logic Pro, the task is accomplished using what is referred to as the *chord grid*. The Score Editor also has symbols for hammers, palms, bends, and more. See Figure 14.14. Generally, you only see the tablature for fret positions in sheet music as an aid to guitarists who are not comfortable with traditional notation, and you see all the other markings only if the composer really knows the guitar (perhaps he is a guitarist) and wants some very specific things. Creating tablature is very doable but also very time-consuming; the manual does a fine job of explaining it, so I will not do that here.

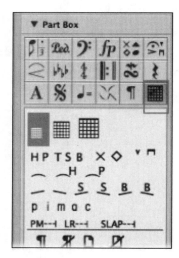

Figure 14.14 Chord Grid symbols in the Part Box.

15 Creating Parts for Specialized Instruments and Instrument Sections

Harp

The harp is another one of those instruments that you have to know quite well to compose well for, especially when coming to grips with the complexity of enharmonic pedaling. Here is an excellent website for learning more about the harp: www.harpspectrum.org/harpworks/ composing_for_harp/composing_for_harp.shtml.

That said, I spent a fair amount of time notating the pedal changes on cues a number of years ago only to be told by the legendary L.A. session harpist Gayle Levant that I needn't bother, because even when it is technically correct, she frequently makes her own choices. (Sigh.) My advice is to learn and understand so you can avoid unknowingly writing parts that are impossible or unmusical, but only mark on the score what the player really needs to see. In Figure 15.1, you can see a little part I played. It begins with a couple of rolled chords and is followed by a broken chord pattern into another rolled chord. At the end I want a glissando, so I have entered the starting note and the ending note.

I need to add arpeggio symbols from the Part Box to the left of the rolled chords. As you can see in Figure 15.2, there are three of them: one without an arrow, one with an up arrow, and one with a down arrow. I want to use the arrowless symbol. But I foresee a problem: The rolled chords on the downbeat of bar 1 and bar 6 simply do not have enough room to the left to display well. The answer is the Layout tool. In fact, much of the time you will be using this tool to adjust note spacing or the number of bars on a given line. I suggest you make it your default Command-key tool for the Score Editor, as I have in Figure 15.3.

Shift-select the rolled chords on the downbeat of bar 1 and bar 6 that I mentioned and, while holding the Command key, use the Layout tool to move them to the right. Now you have room for the arpeggio symbols, as you see in Figure 15.4.

1. Drag the arpeggio symbol into bar 1. Then use the Pointer tool to grab the very top of the symbol and drag it up so it is the length of the rolled chord. See Figure 15.5.

2. Option-drag the symbol to bar 6. The result is seen in Figure 15.6.

Figure 15.1 A simple harp part in Page View.

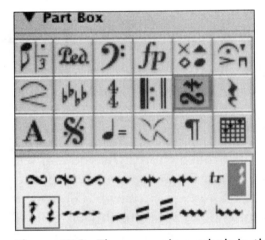

Figure 15.2 The arpeggio symbols in the Part Box.

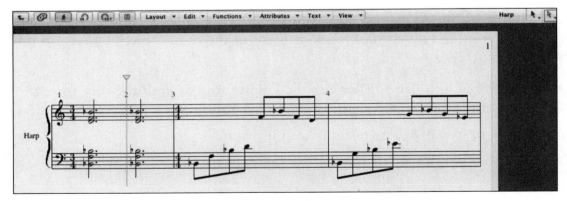

Figure 15.3 The Layout tool assigned to be the command tool.

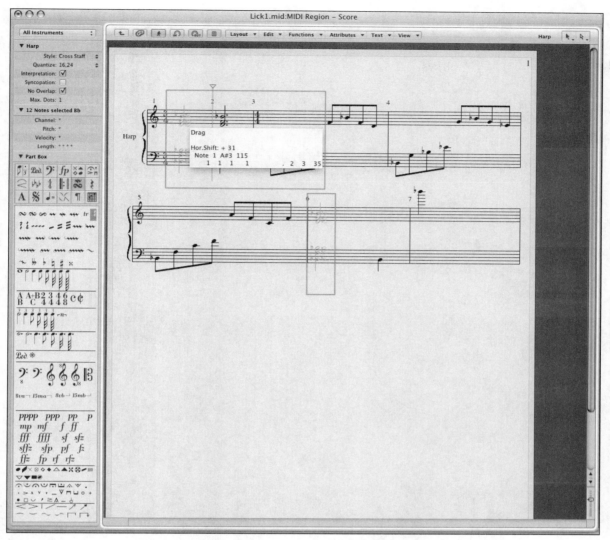

Figure 15.4   Using the Layout tool to create space for the arpeggio symbols.

It is time to deal with the glissando. Once again there are multiple possible symbol choices for drawing lines, as you see in Figure 15.7. You are going to use the one that slants upward.

1.   Drag the symbol from the Part Box to beat 4 of bar 6. When you release the mouse, you can see that the symbol is straight across, even though you chose the symbol that slants upward. See Figure 15.8.

2.   Grab the handle on the right side of the line and drag it up; see Figure 15.9. In Figure 15.10, it appears as you want it to. All you need to do is to add the text "glissando" or "gliss," slurs, and dynamics. Figure 15.11 shows you are good to go with the harp part. (Sadly, Logic cannot do rotated text.)

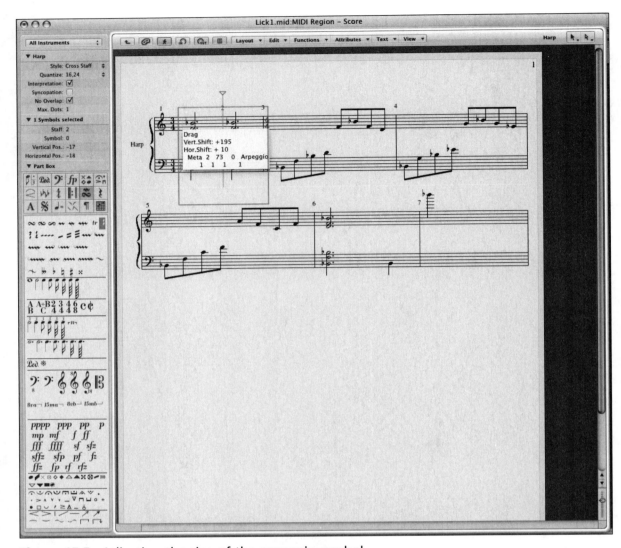

Figure 15.5 Adjusting the size of the arpeggio symbol.

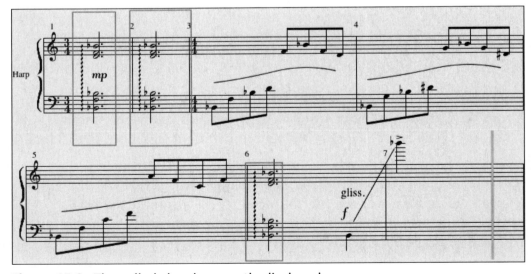

Figure 15.6 The rolled chords correctly displayed.

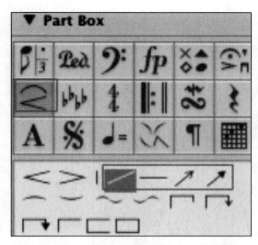

Figure 15.7 The glissando symbols.

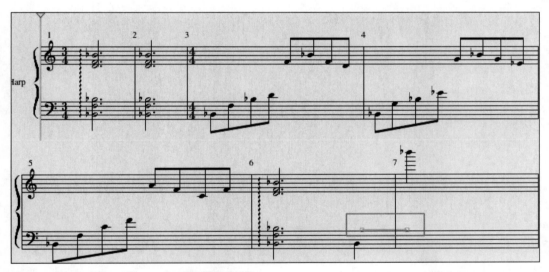

Figure 15.8 The glissando symbol is flat.

Converting a Region Played as Chords to Separate Parts

While I almost always play my parts discretely, composers commonly use some kind of combo horn or string patch and play a part as chords that must eventually end up as separate parts. In Figure 15.12, I am showing a swing part for horns that I played in (commonly referred to at schools like Berklee College of Music as *four-way close* writing). I used a combo sax patch but I need this to split out to parts for two altos, one tenor, and one baritone sax.

Logic can help with this. It looks at all the top notes and assigns them (or keeps them) at channel 1. Then it looks to find a line of notes below those pitches and assigns them to channel 2 and so on.

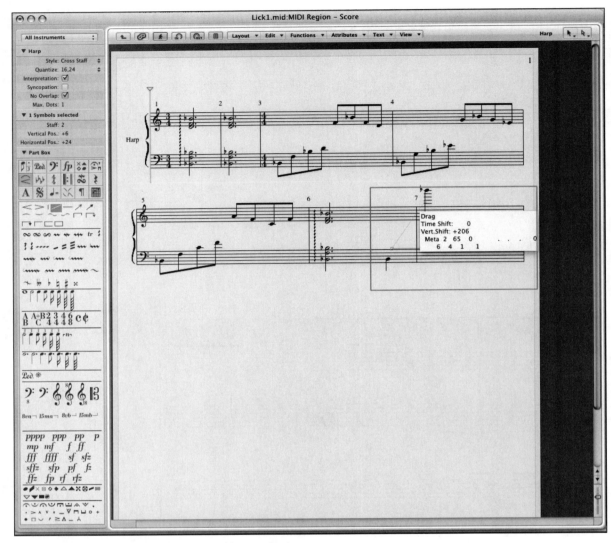

Figure 15.9   Adjusting the glissando symbol.

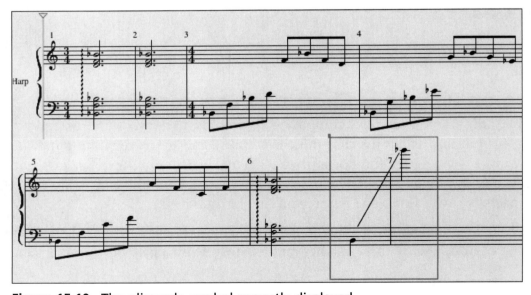

Figure 15.10   The glissando symbol correctly displayed.

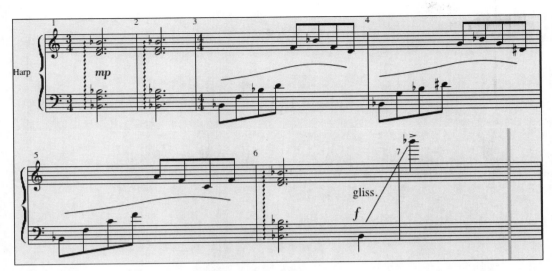

Figure 15.11   The completed harp part.

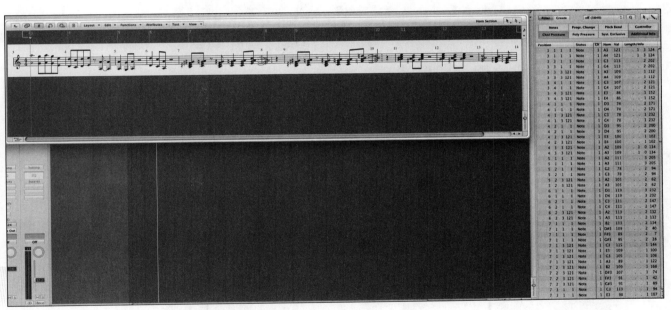

Figure 15.12   A swing part for a sax section.

In the case of the octaves at the beginning of the piece, Logic will only detect two voices (so notes will be assigned to channels 1 and 2). But once it gets to the chords, it will detect four voices (channels 1–4).

Notice in Figure 15.12 that in the Event List, all voices are assigned to the internal MIDI channel 1.

1. In the Score Editor, press Command-A to ensure that all the notes are selected.

2. Under the Functions menu, choose Note Events > Voices to Channels. The notes are distributed between MIDI channels 1–4. See Figure 15.13.

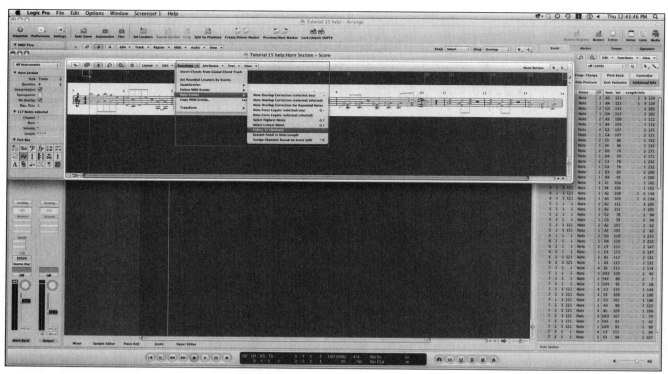

Figure 15.13 Performing Voices to Channels.

3. In the Arrange Window, choose MIDI > Separate MIDI Events > By Event Channel, as you see in Figure 15.14. The result is shown in Figure 15.15: four separate regions.

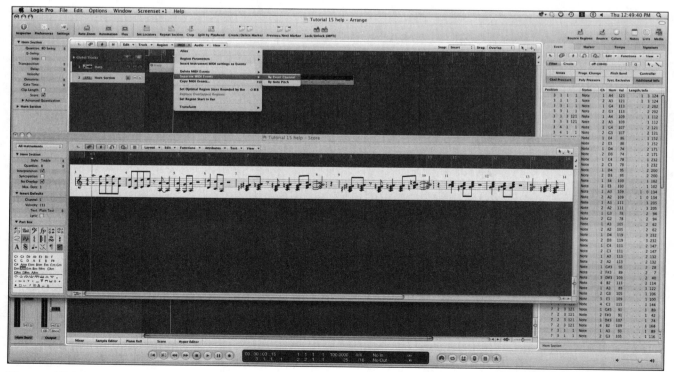

Figure 15.14 Separating by event channel.

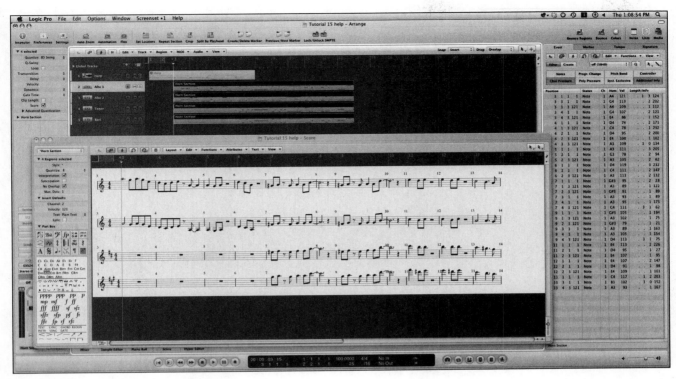

Figure 15.15   Four separate regions.

All that needs to be done from my standpoint as an arranger working in four-way close writing is to copy the alto notes in the first four bars into the tenor and baritone regions in the octave I want them played; I need to assign each region to the proper staff style. This assignment is pretty easy because Logic has default staff styles for alto, tenor, and baritone sax. As you can see in Figure 15.16, it is ready to add any dynamics and articulations.

Figure 15.16   The discrete sax parts assigned to the proper transposed staff styles.

16 Getting to Know the Score Preferences and Project Settings

The Score Preferences Window

As with all Logic Pro 9 preferences, any changes you make are global to the program and will affect projects created in the past, present, and future. Your mileage, as they say, may vary. In Figure 16.1, you can see the Preferences Window. That's it for the score preferences. Notice the Score Project Settings button in the lower-right corner. Clicking it will take you directly to the Score project settings, where there are many choices you can make, as discussed in the next few sections.

Display

You'll find the following options in the Display area of the Preferences Window.

- **Show Region Selection Colored:** If you check this box, the staff lines of the currently selected MIDI region are shown in blue (all others are black). This distinction helps ensure that any adjustments you make in the Display Parameter Box are for the desired regions.

- **Display Distance Values in Inches:** When you check this box, the measurement units in the project settings and page rulers in Page View are in inches (rather than the default of centimeters). If, like many Americans, you have not yet made friends with the metric system, this could be helpful to you.

- **Floating Palette View:** If you double-click a part group in the Part Box, a floating palette displays the member of that group. If the palette is set to Standard, Logic decides whether it is best displayed horizontally or vertically. If you choose Horizontal or Vertical, the palette appears in accordance with your choice. See Figure 16.2. Standard has always been fine for me.

- **Double-Click Note to Open:** This defaults to opening a window that you see in Figure 16.3. Here you can override choices you may have made or that Logic is making for you for a specific note. Alternatively, you can have Logic open the Event List, Piano Roll Editor, or Hyper Editor.

- **Selection Color:** You can change the color of selected objects in the Score Editor by double-clicking the palette and clicking a color; the default is green. Clicking Reset returns it to green.

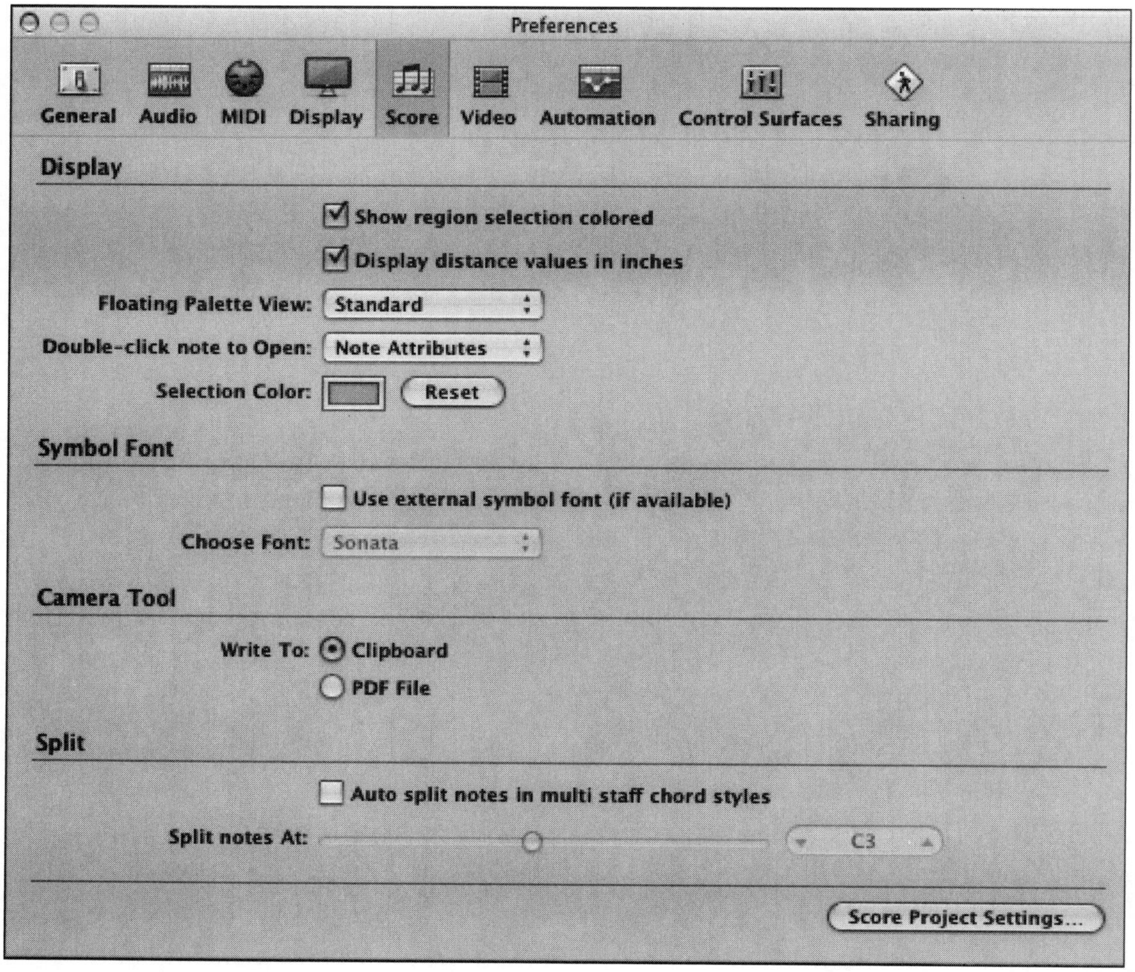

Figure 16.1　The Preferences Window.

Symbol Font

Some third-party symbol fonts can be purchased for use with Logic—such as Adobe's Sonata and Sigler Music's Jazz and Swing fonts. In Figure 16.4, you can see a comparison of Logic's font with Sonata. In Figure 16.5, you can see the Jazz and Swing fonts. While they are cool alternatives, updates to Logic and the Mac OS sometimes have made their use dicey, as what appears on the screen can create a corrupted printout or PDF. Caveat emptor.

Camera Tool

If you want to export images from the score with the Camera tool, you can do so via the clipboard or as a PDF. However, while this is a great concept, in my experience, using it only results in frustration; sadly, it simply does not work as it should.

Figure 16.2 Vertical and horizontal floating palettes of a group in the Part Box.

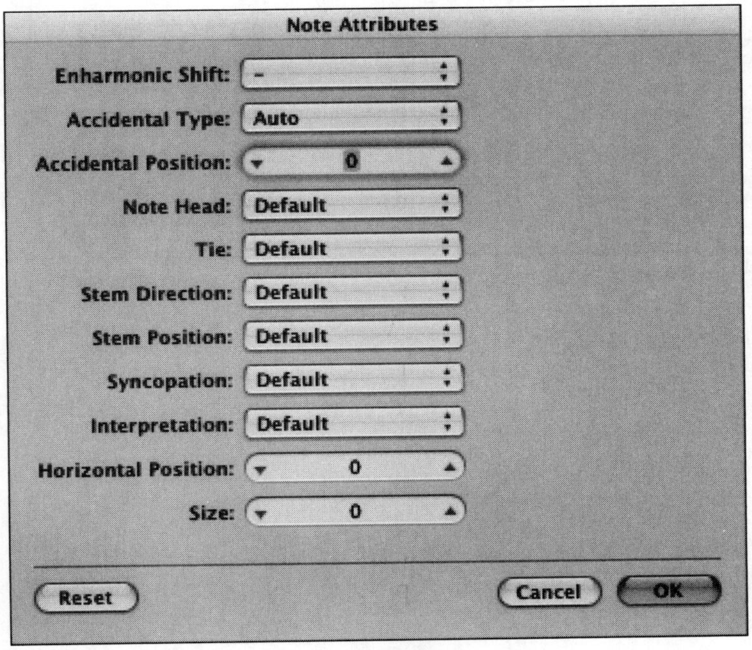

Note Attributes

Enharmonic Shift: –

Accidental Type: Auto

Accidental Position: ▼ 0 ▲

Note Head: Default

Tie: Default

Stem Direction: Default

Stem Position: Default

Syncopation: Default

Interpretation: Default

Horizontal Position: ▼ 0 ▲

Size: ▼ 0 ▲

Reset   Cancel   OK

Figure 16.3 The Note Attributes Window.

Figure 16.4 Logic's font (top) and the Sonata font from Adobe (bottom).

Figure 16.5 The Jazz and Swing fonts from Sigler Music.

Split

Auto Split Notes in Multi-Staff Chord Styles is only relevant for Polyphonic staff styles using MIDI channels for voice assignment, such as Piano 1/3. If you check this box, the Split Notes At slider draws in the chosen split point.

The Score Editor's Project Settings

When you open the Score project settings, you are presented with an impressive and perhaps daunting set of choices that are specific to the current project. See Figure 16.6.

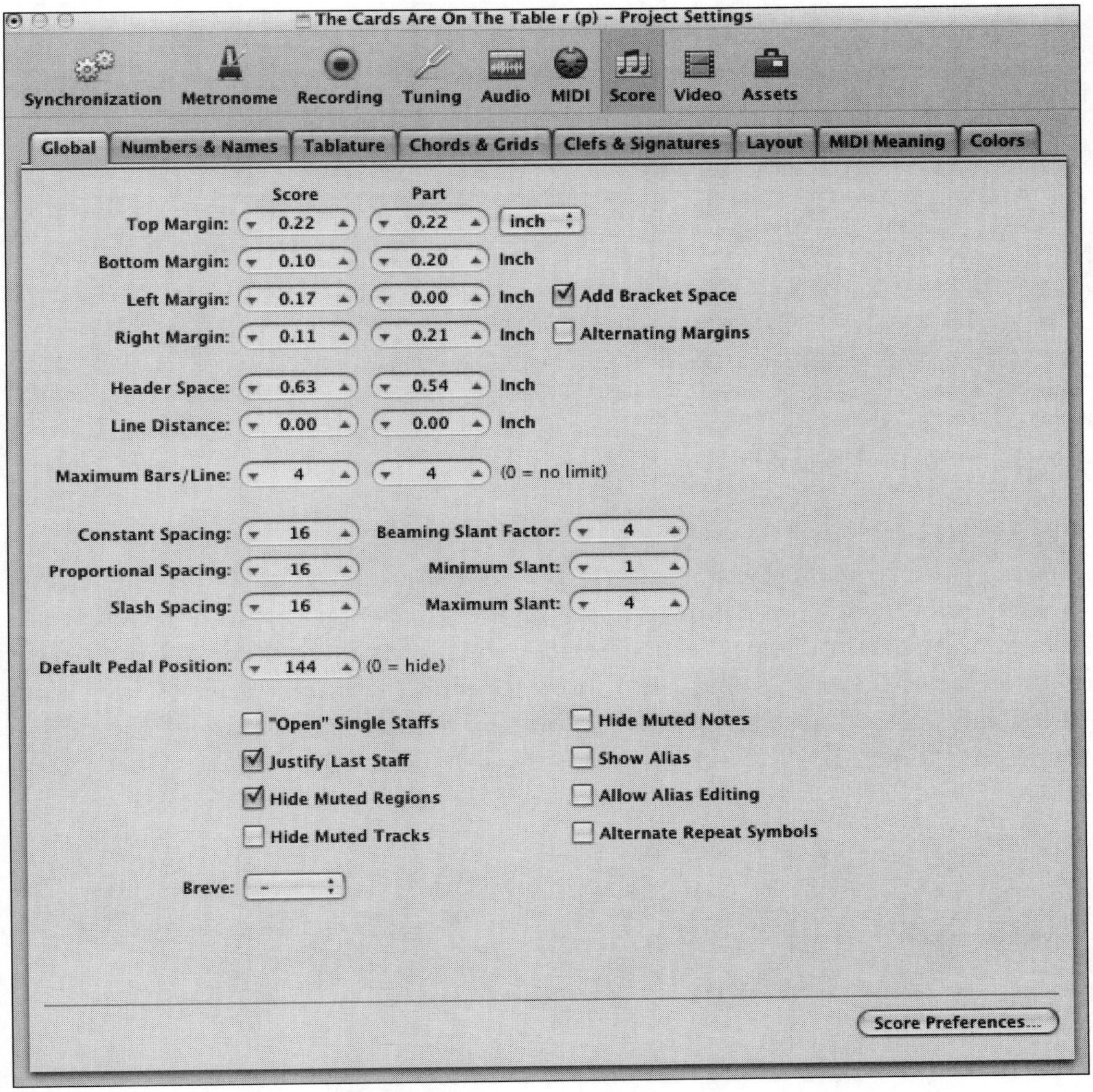

Figure 16.6 The Project Settings Window.

The manual uses 22 pages to explain the Score Project Settings options, so refer to the manual for more in-depth information. Here I will highlight some of those I deem most important. Every long-time score user has his own favorite settings. Trial and error (hopefully not while you are doing paying work) is the only real way to make your decisions. Be aware that, while these settings are not global to Logic Pro, they *are* global to all score sets in the project. Make sure to choose View > Page View > Print View for this tutorial, as these settings are primarily about how things look on a printed page. See Figure 16.7.

Figure 16.7   Print View in Page Display Options.

There are eight tabs, as you can see in Figure 16.8. In the Global group, you can decide whether to display certain settings in inches or centimeters; see Figure 16.9. You can have different settings for the full score and parts. I always keep separate projects for these because I print parts and full scores on different size papers; going back and forth with the printer driver setting leads me to make mistakes. But these choices do exist, and you may decide that you prefer one project for both the full score and the parts.

Figure 16.8   The eight categories of Score Project Settings.

Note   If you do prefer to work in one project, know that the Score settings affect the layout of the music only if a score set other than the default All Instruments is selected. Part settings affect the layout of the music only if the default All Instruments score set is selected or if you are viewing a part as selected via Logic's part-extraction feature (Option-click in the score set). But I do not personally recommend this workflow.

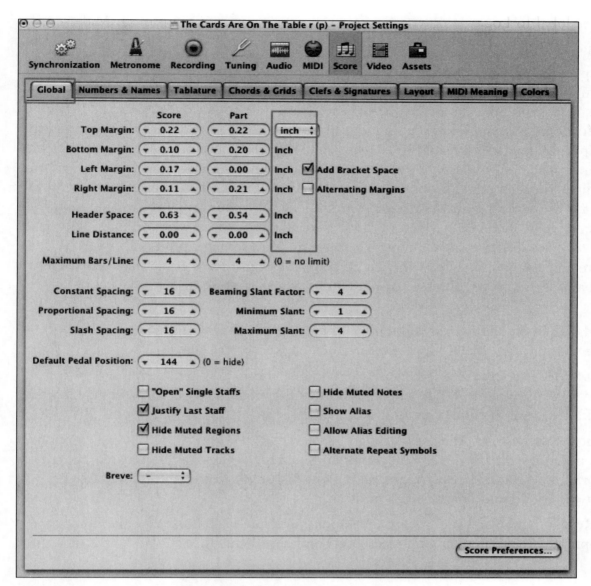

Figure 16.9   Choosing inches or centimeters for adjustments.

Global

You can safely leave most of these settings at the default, but some can have rather dramatic consequences.

- **Header Space and Line Distance:** These settings can be especially important in a large full score. You cannot generally leave as much space between staves after the first page without sacrificing fitting them on the first page. After experimenting with these settings, you can usually find an acceptable compromise. Sometimes, however, I print the first page looking as I like it, change the settings, and then print out the subsequent pages. There is merit in the idea of saving a version that works well for the first page under one file name, and then saving under a different file name a version that works well for the subsequent pages.

- **Maximum Bars/Line:** This setting can be important, although, as I discuss in the next tutorial, you can override it by using the Layout tool to change line breaks.

- **Constant Spacing and Proportional Spacing:** Tweaking these settings can be a huge problem solver. I simply cannot explain this better or more succinctly than the manual, so I am going to quote it: "Constant Spacing affects the distance from note to note, regardless of rhythmic value. Proportional Spacing takes the note durations into consideration. If you only use Proportional Spacing (and set Constant to 0), every bar receives (more or less) the same amount of (horizontal) space. A whole note uses as much space as four quarter notes. In the opposite situation (high constant value, proportional value set to 0), the distance from one note to the next is always the same, regardless of note duration. A half note takes the same amount of space as an eighth note. Other factors, such as accidentals, ties, and so on, are also considered for note distance calculations. The settings you use depend on both your personal preference and the style of the piece. You should aim for a good balance between these two parameters, so try different combinations when working on the final score layout."

- **Default Pedal Position:** Setting this option to 0 hides the pedal symbols that may have affected the sound of the MIDI but do not need to be seen by the player.

- **Justify Last Staff:** This option lengthens the last line or last staff system in full scores and parts to the right page margin. I generally leave this box unchecked, as it is a simple matter to use the Layout tool to countermand it when necessary.

- **Hiding Muted Regions and Aliases:** I strongly recommend that you render all these options moot by converting your aliases to real copies and merging regions, as I discussed in an earlier tutorial, and simply delete the muted regions (assuming you are keeping different projects for the sound and for the score printout).

- **Alternate Repeat Symbols:** Make repeat signs look more like Real Book or Fake Book style with this option. I check this only on lead sheets and chord charts.

Numbers & Names Group

The Numbers & Names group is very important (for me). I make very different choices with the settings in this group for parts than I do for full scores, which is another reason I keep separate projects for each.

- **Page Numbers:** I like them to alternate from left to right at the top of the page in parts, with the first page number hidden. See Figure 16.10. However, on full scores I prefer page numbers to be centered, at the bottom, with a prefix. I can achieve that with the settings you see in Figure 16.11. All these choices are, of course, highly subjective and there is no "right" way to do this.

- **Bar Numbers:** Once again, I make quite different choices for parts versus full scores. On parts, I prefer bar numbers at the bar line but below the staff, and for only the first bar of

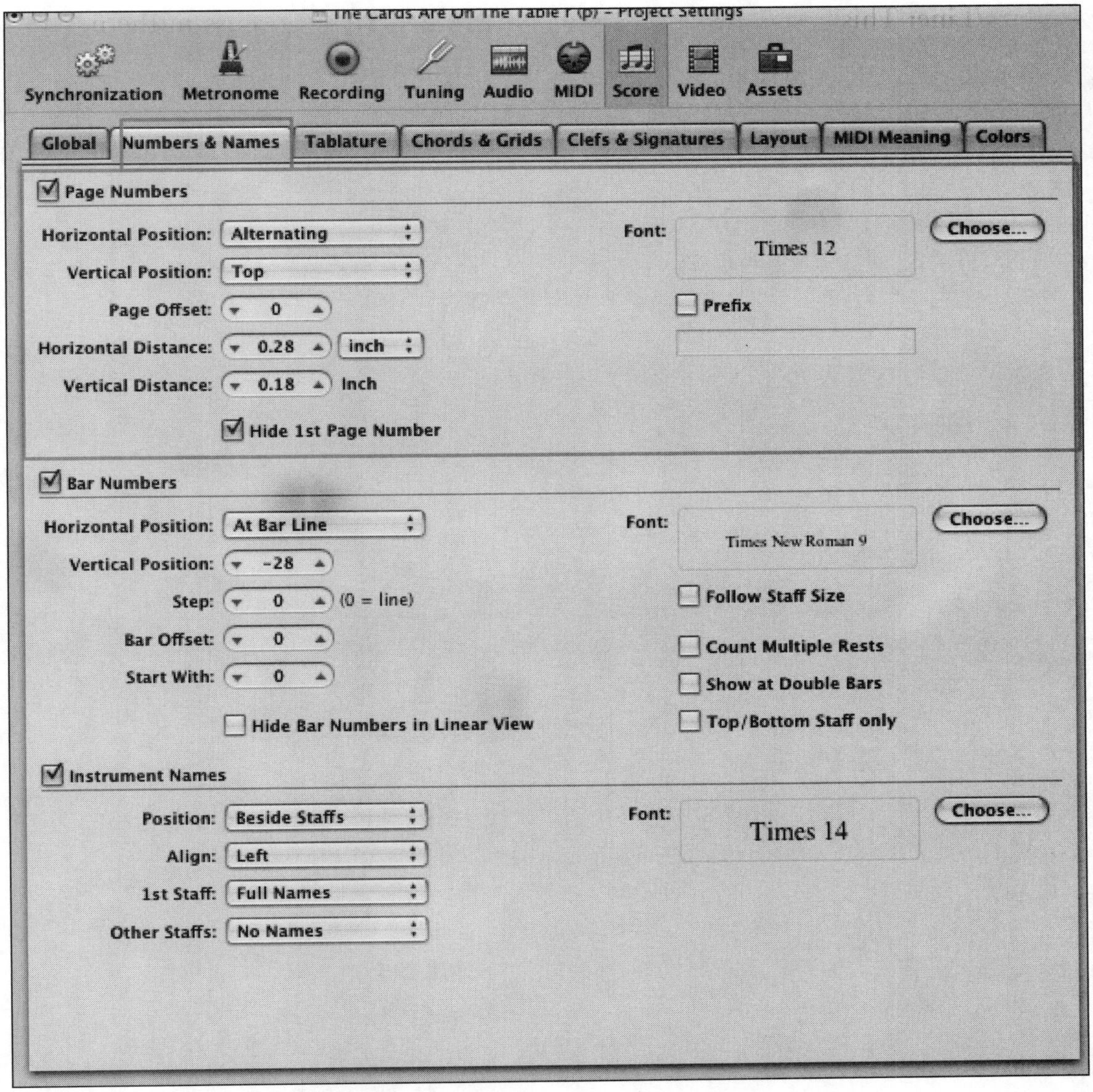

Figure 16.10   Page Numbers settings for parts.

each line to be displayed. I can achieve this by setting Vertical Position to a negative value and setting Step to 0. See Figure 16.12. However, in a full score I want them for every bar, circled, and appearing between sections of the orchestra/band (as you can see in Figure 16.13). To achieve this, I need to have created a Text style that is circled, I need the settings shown in Figure 16.14, and I need to draw in the bracket breaks that you see in Figure 16.15.

■ **Instrument Names:** The only difference between parts and the full score is that, for parts, I want to see the name on the first staff; see Figure 16.16. On the full score, I want to see

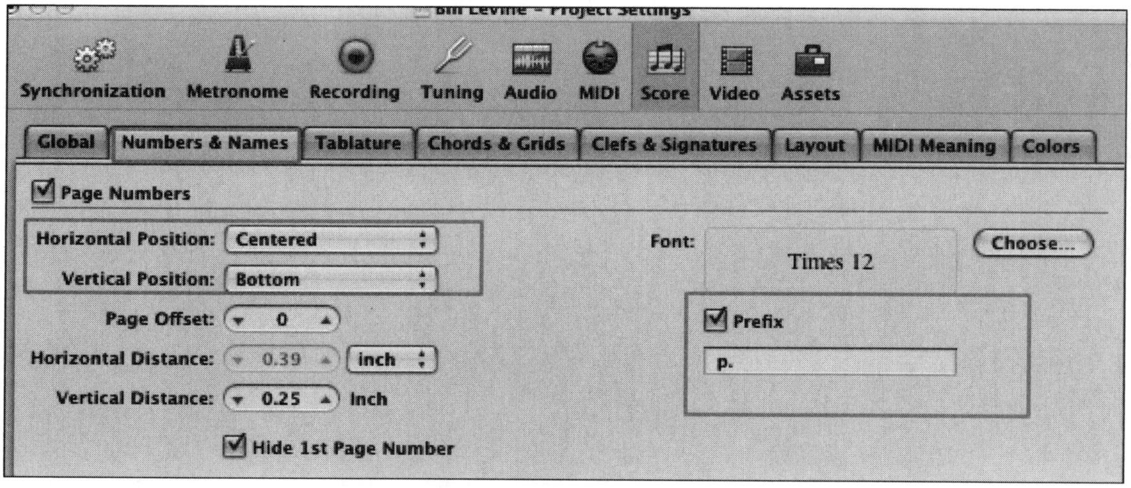

Figure 16.11 Page Numbers settings for full scores.

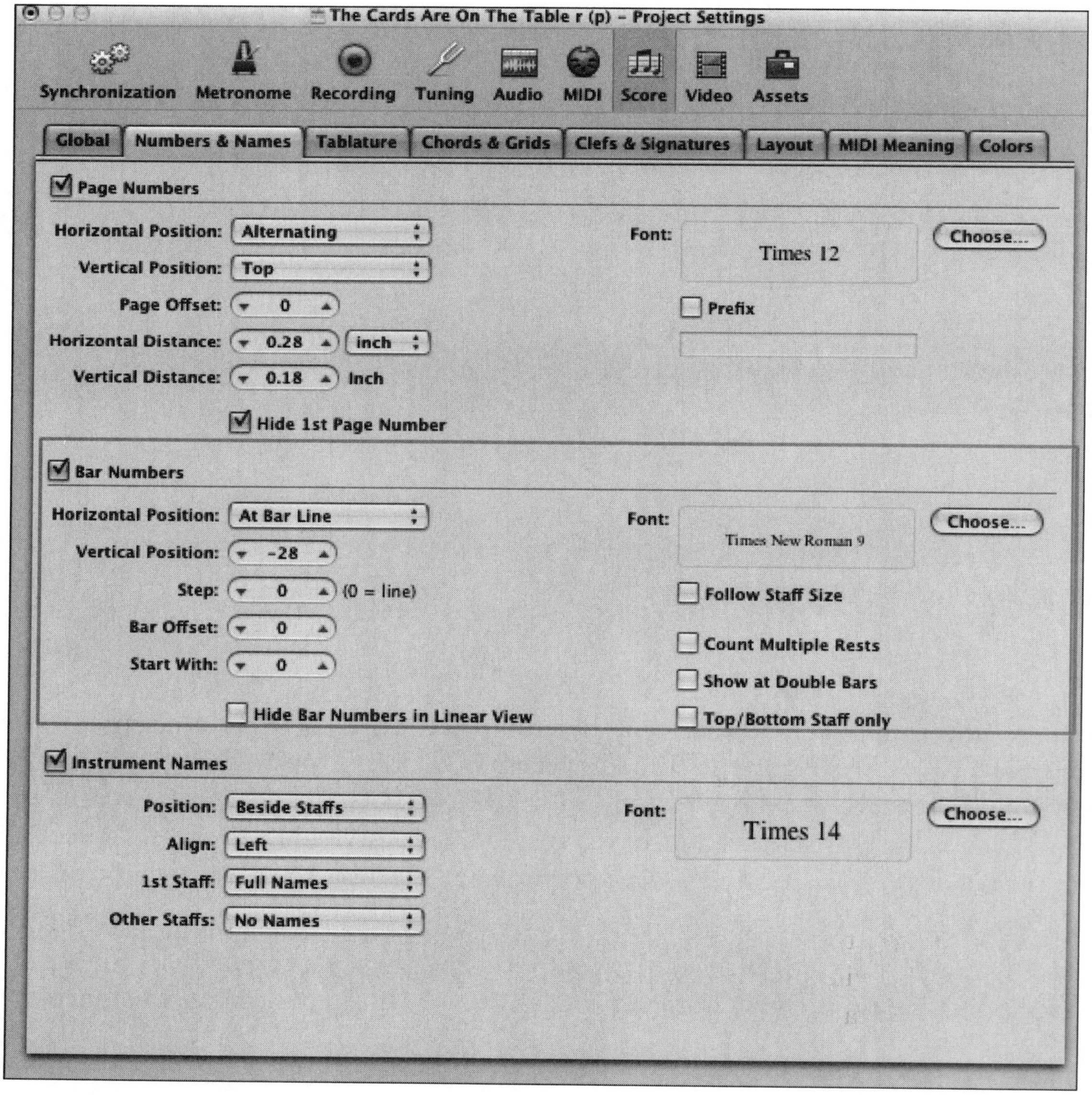

Figure 16.12 Bar Numbers settings for parts.

Figure 16.13 A full score with the bar numbers as I like them to be displayed.

the full name on the first staff and a short name that I have entered in the score set on the subsequent staffs.

Tablature

In Figure 16.17 you can see the Tablature group settings. As I wrote in Tutorial 14, tablature is an alternative way of displaying guitar parts that is not used in traditional notation and requires a deep understanding of guitar technique. The manual explains it very well.

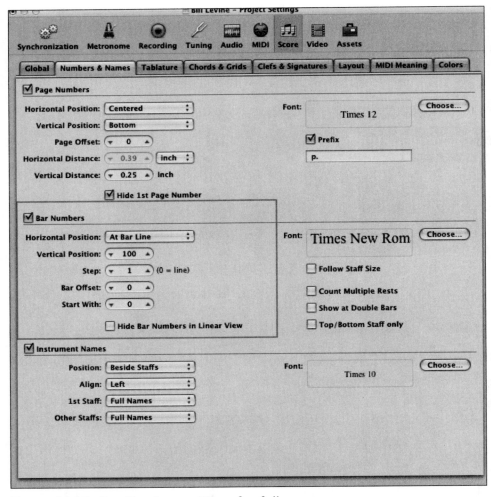

Figure 16.14 Bar Numbers settings for full scores.

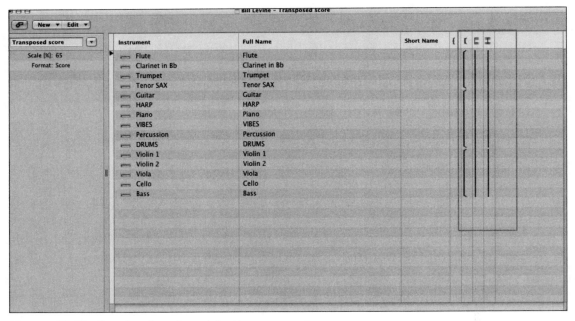

Figure 16.15 Bracket breaks set in the score set.

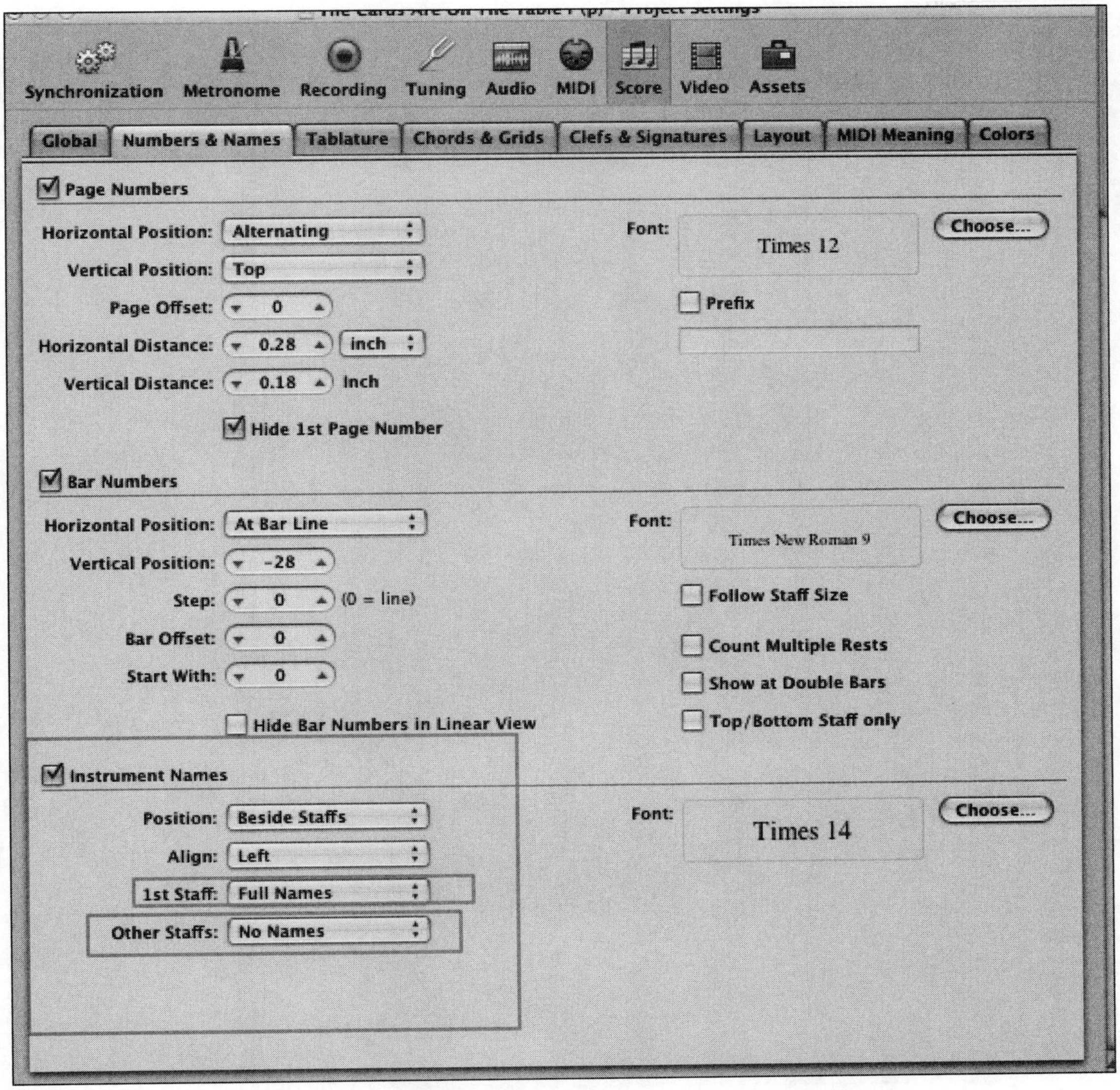

Figure 16.16 Instrument Names settings for parts.

Chords & Grids

In Figure 16.18, you can see the Chords & Grids group settings and a guitar part. In the Chords area, I usually deviate from the defaults by checking Follow Staff Size; also, I like them to be center aligned. Grids, like tablature, are another kind of guitar notation that I have never been called upon to use. It is mostly used in commercially released sheet music for guitar. Once again, should you wish to utilize it, the manual explains it well.

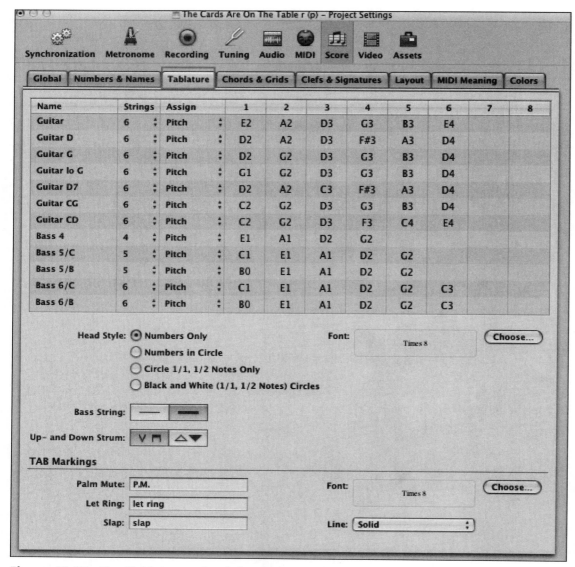

Figure 16.17 The Tablature tab of the Project Settings Window.

Clefs & Signatures

In Figure 16.19, you can see the Clefs & Signatures group settings and an accordion part. The only change I have ever felt compelled to make to the defaults is for the Smaller Clef Change option, which only affects those clefs dragged into the score from the Part Box and not the clef at the beginning of each line. I prefer all clefs in a part to be the same size, but frankly, leaving it at the default of −2 would not keep me awake at night.

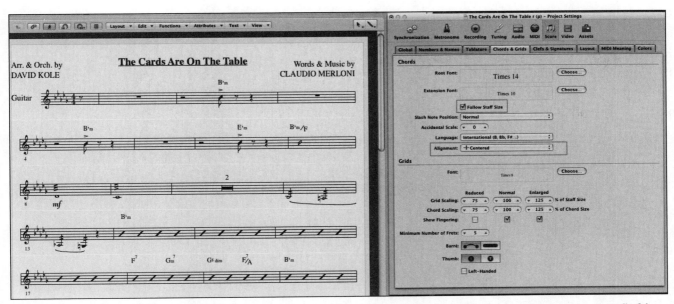

Figure 16.18 The Chords & Grids group (right) of the Project Settings Window and a guitar part (left).

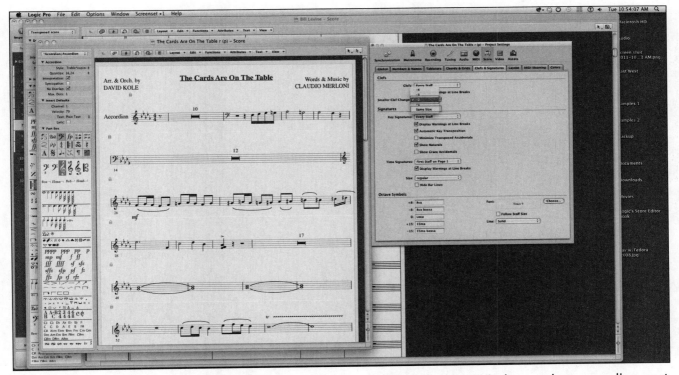

Figure 16.19 The Clefs & Signatures group (right) of the Project Settings Window and an accordion part (left).

Layout

In Figure 16.20, you can see the Layout group of the Project Settings Window. Changing these *has* kept me awake at night. I am almost constantly changing them (especially those in the Others area), and then changing my mind again and again. Thank heavens for the Factory Defaults button in the lower-right corner. Clicking it bails me out when I have royally screwed up by too many experiments with slur thickness, etc.

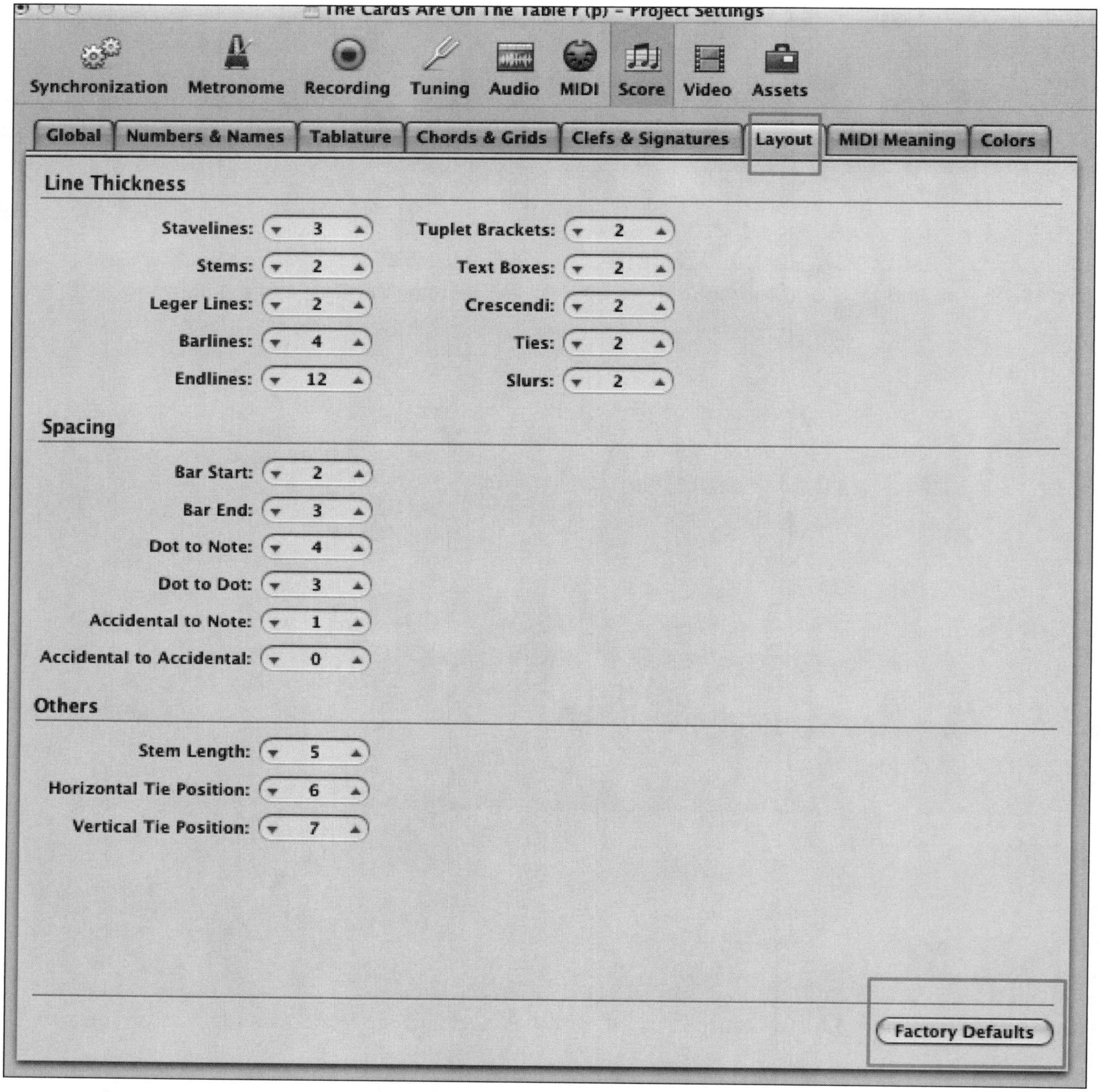

Figure 16.20 The Layout group of the Project Settings Window.

MIDI Meaning

The MIDI Meaning group that you see in Figure 16.21 allows certain symbols to actually alter the length of notes to which they're applied. Any changes to the settings must be made *before* you insert the symbols. To use a symbol again normally (no length change), its value must first be reset to the default of 100%.

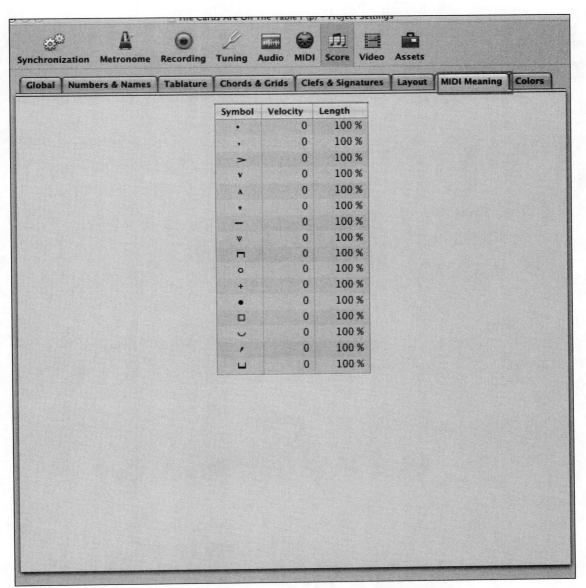

Symbol	Velocity	Length
.	0	100 %
.	0	100 %
>	0	100 %
∨	0	100 %
∧	0	100 %
▾	0	100 %
—	0	100 %
v	0	100 %
⊓	0	100 %
o	0	100 %
+	0	100 %
●	0	100 %
▢	0	100 %
⌣	0	100 %
╱	0	100 %
⊔	0	100 %

Figure 16.21 The MIDI Meaning group of the Project Settings Window.

Colors

The Colors group of the Project Settings Window (shown in Figure 16.22) is useful for earlier editing and for educational scores and parts instruction, but not in any professional score preparation job.

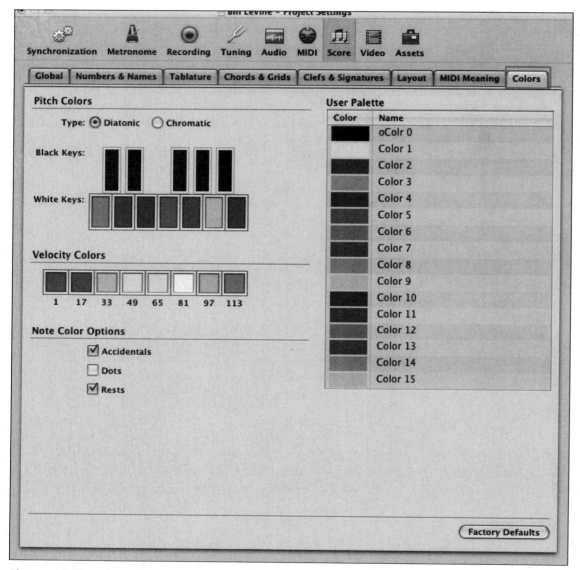

Figure 16.22 The Colors group of the Project Settings Window.

17 Layout Techniques for Scores

Score First, Then Parts? Or Parts First, Then Score?

Should you tend to the score first, then the parts, or tend to the parts first, then the score? Arguments can be made each way. On the surface, it seems logical to do the score first, because changes are automatically made in the parts. (Indeed, many score programs traditionally use the method of preparing the full score and then "extracting" the parts.) That approach is fine if you only use one project for the full score and the parts—although, even with that methodology, changes can so alter your layout that much of the work has to be redone anyway. And what if you are preparing a concert score without the instrument transpositions because that is what the conductor (or you) wants to look at during the recording session? Or what if you keep a separate project for each? No matter how you look at it, extensive changes mean pain. In Logic Pro 9, however, you can import regions from one project to another; that makes changes much less painful. Deciding whether to go score first or parts first becomes a matter of user preference. In this chapter I do the full score first, using a cue from a score for the film *Slap Her, She's French* by David Michael Frank (for which I did the score prep).

In Figure 17.1, you can see the Arrange Window. I already performed many of the steps that I suggest in Tutorial 3. All the regions are the length of the cue, all muted regions are gone, and all extraneous parts that are not performed live are either deleted or hidden. It is lean and mean.

Because I always print full scores on legal-sized paper, I first make sure that what I will be viewing in Logic's score reflects that size destination. With the Score Window open, go to the Page Setup Window and make sure Legal Size is selected. Sadly, you have to change the paper size when you prepare parts to print on letter-sized paper. Logic cannot save these settings with a project. See Figures 17.2 and 17.3.

This is not a huge orchestra, but take a look at Figure 17.4: the entire set of instruments is not visible in the Score Editor. You need to scale the score set.

1. In the Inspector, double-click the score set. See Figure 17.5.

2. Make an educated guess about how to scale the score set. In this example I chose 60%, and as you can see in Figure 17.6, I can see nearly all the instruments.

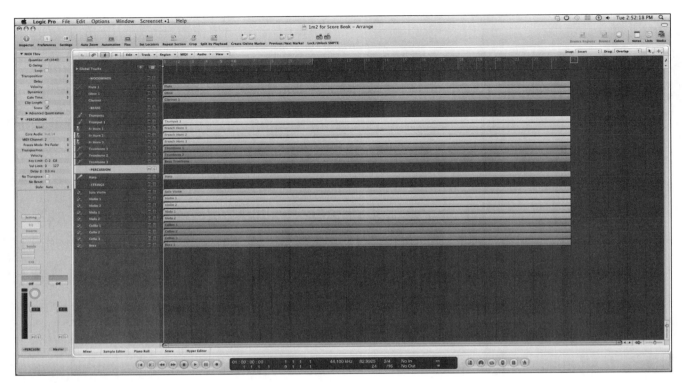

Figure 17.1 The 1m2 Arrange Window.

I could scale it to a smaller percentage, but I see a lot of space between the instrument staves. I could tighten up the space quite a bit, which I think is preferable to scaling again. The problem is, frequently several instruments are assigned to the same staff style; adjusting the spacing of one will affect them all. For instance, the flute and the oboe are assigned to Treble staff style. If I want to move the oboe closer to the flute without affecting the latter's appearance and spacing, I need to duplicate the staff style for the flute and perhaps for the oboe as well.

1. Hold the mouse down on the Treble staff style and, as shown in Figure 17.7, navigate down to **** DUPLICATE!****. It creates a staff style named Treble Copied.

2. Double-click the style to open it and rename it Flute. See Figure 17.8.

Here is another method for duplicating staff styles:

1. While still in the staff style you want to copy, choose New > Duplicate Staff Style. The staff style I want to copy in this case is Flute; see Figure 17.9.

2. Rename the style (Oboe in this example) and change its upper and lower Space settings. In this example, I changed the settings from 145 and 72 to 70 and 70; see Figure 17.10.

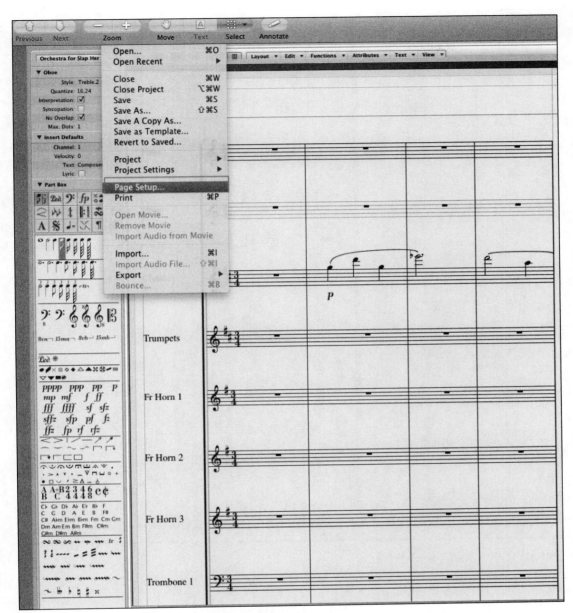

Figure 17.2 Opening the Page Setup Window.

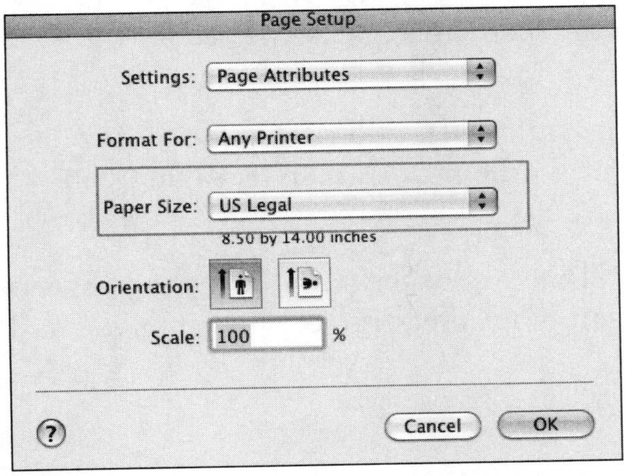

Figure 17.3 Setting Paper Size to US Legal in the Page Setup Window.

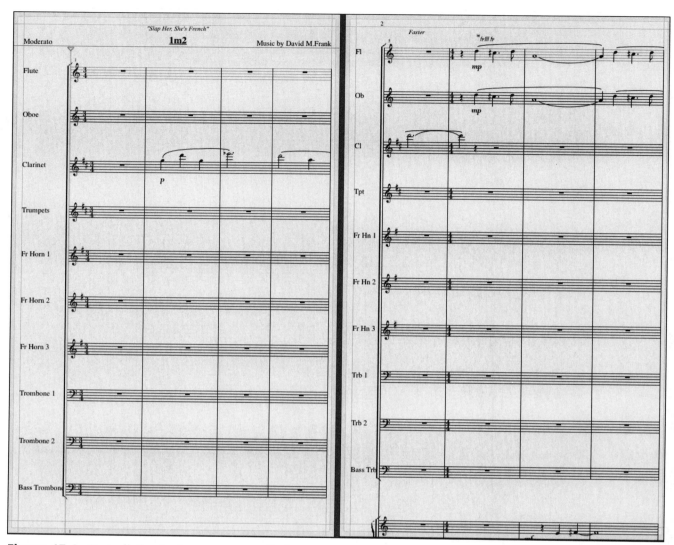

Figure 17.4 Not all the instruments are displayed.

3. Close the window and assign the desired region to the newly copied staff style. In this example, it's Flute and Oboe, and the spacing in the score appears as you see in Figure 17.11. Much better.

    If you choose the part first before duplicating the staff style, and then use either of the duplication methods, the part will be assigned to the new staff style, saving you a step.

Now it is a matter of creating individual staff styles for all the rest of the parts. The good news is that once you create these styles, you can import them into your other projects or templates and never have to do much of this again. Take heart.

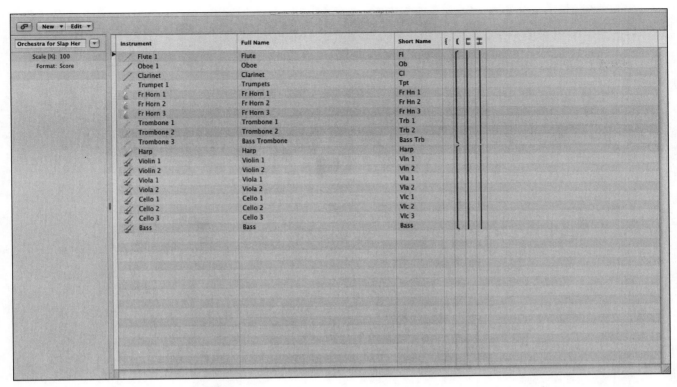

Figure 17.5   Opening the score set.

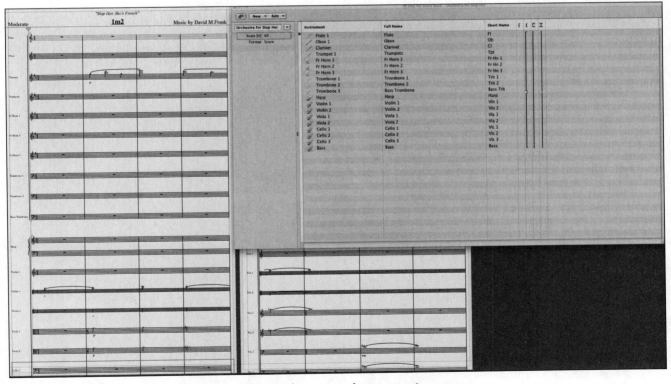

Figure 17.6   Scaling the score set to 60% makes more instruments appear.

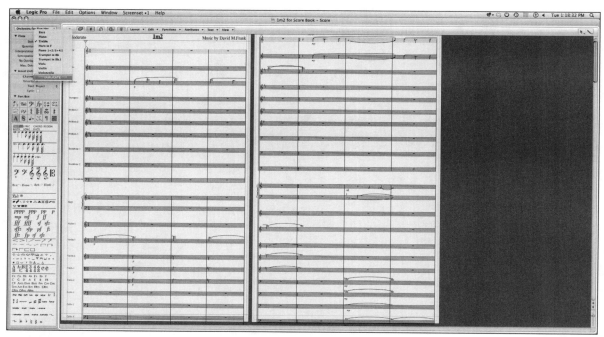

Figure 17.7 Duplicating the Treble staff style.

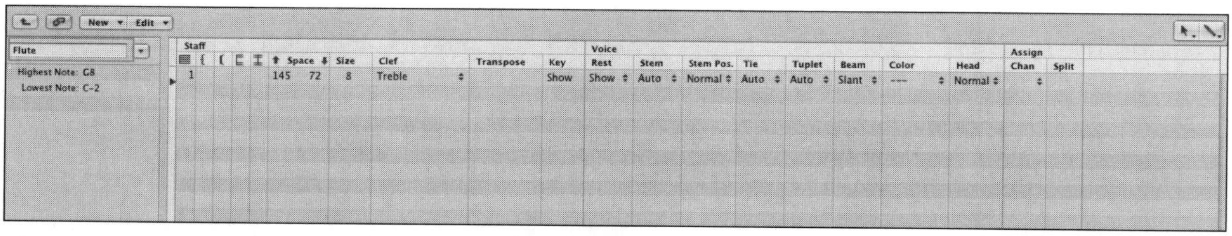

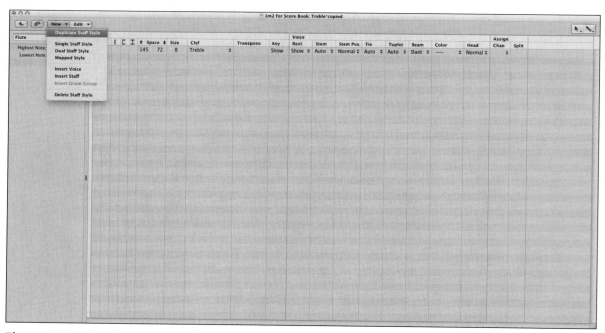

Figure 17.8 Renaming the duplicated staff style.

Figure 17.9 Duplicating a staff style from within a staff style.

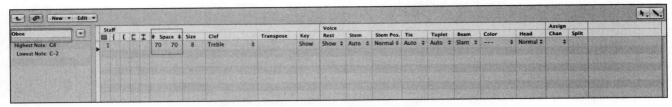

Figure 17.10 Changing the Space setting in the Oboe staff style.

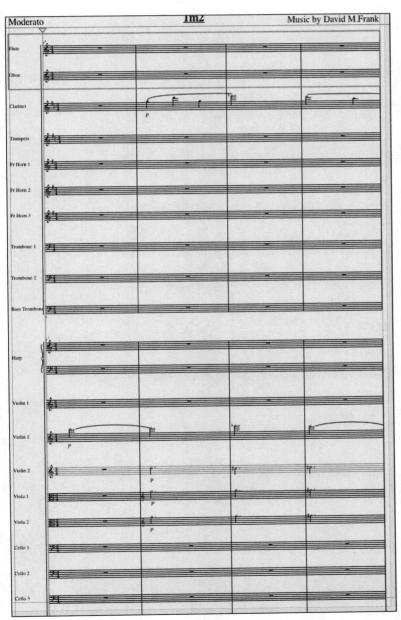

Figure 17.11 Better spacing in the score with the flute and oboe each assigned to an individual staff style.

Clarinet is assigned to the Trumpet in Bb staff style, so I need to do one for it. There are three separate French horns, so I need two duplicates for their spacing. I need Violin, Viola, and Violoncello staff styles, as well as duplicates of the Bass staff style (for the trombones). Once I create and assign all the styles, I do not necessarily have to change the Space settings within them. Instead, I can grab the clef (as shown in Figure 17.12) and drag it up or down.

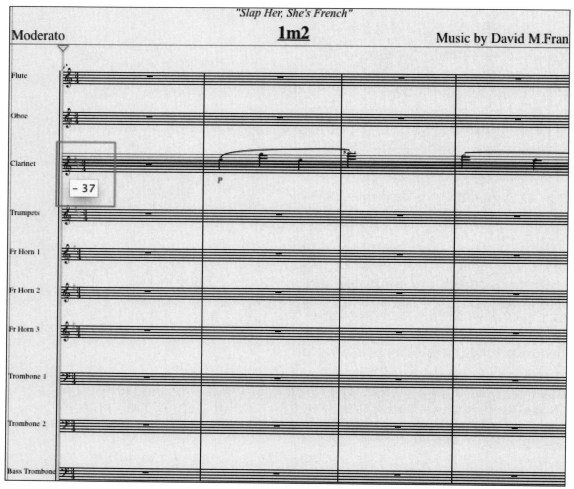

Figure 17.12 Repositioning the clarinet in the score by dragging the clef.

After you reposition, revisit the score set scale and see if you can make it a little bigger. In this cue, I was able to increase the scale percentage to 62%. The final product is in Figure 17.13.

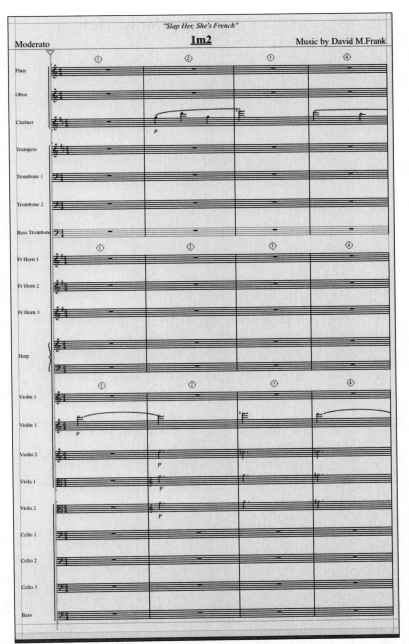

Figure 17.13 The first page of the score after repositioning and rescaling.

Using the Layout Tool

The Layout tool (see Figure 17.14) is wonderful for adjusting a score's layout because it allows you to move measures from one system to another. The line break and page break symbols are. . .err. . .less wonderful (see Figure 17.15). In fact, the symbols are so flawed that I simply cannot recommend using them, as they are too unpredictable. Hopefully, they will be fixed in a future update.

Figure 17.14 Designating the Layout tool as the Command tool in the Score Editor.

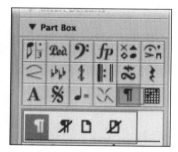

Figure 17.15 Line and page break symbols in the Part Box.

If you have not already done so, assign the Command tool to the Layout tool. In Figure 17.15, you can see the following symbols in the Part Box: Line Break, No Line Break, Page Break, and No Page Break.

In the project settings, I set my default maximum bars to 4. Overall that setting works well, but sometimes I want fewer or more than Logic thinks is desirable. Here is where the Layout tool is very nifty. Unfortunately, I cannot show exactly what I would like you to see because the cursor is not included in a screenshot when you take one.

I hold the Command key and choose the fifth measure. In Figure 17.16, you can see the help tag titled Move Bars. It appears and the cursor changes to a hand (though you cannot see that here). Then I simply drag measure five up to the preceding line and it now has five measures. I do this for the rest of the score.

Figure 17.16 Moving bars with the Layout tool.

However, if I revisit an earlier page and change the number of bars in a line, all the subsequent changes are nullified and return to the defaults. Now you must redo the resulting layout that occurs after you change the lines. You need to be methodical about this, one page at a time, starting with the first line on each page and working down.

Editing Margins and Header Values and Printing or Exporting the Score

You can easily edit headers and margins if they are visible. To make them all visible, select Show Margins under View > Page Display Options. Now the margins and the header are visible, as shown in Figure 17.17.

- Grab the orange line to drag the margin to the right of the default printer margin.

- Grab the purple line to drag the header down to make its space bigger.

When your score looks as you like it, you can simply print it. (I print on legal-sized paper and have a copy store blow it up onto 11 × 17" paper, but if you have invested in a large-format printer, you are ahead of the game.)

You can export the score as a graphic file (like a PDF), or copy it to the clipboard and paste it into another application for further work. You can use the Camera tool for this task

Figure 17.17 Making the margin and header lines visible.

theoretically, but as I said in Tutorial 16, it is very buggy and erratic and I cannot recommend you doing so. A better solution is to press Command-P for printing and select PDF > Save as PDF. See Figure 17.18. Alternatively you can use the Mac's various screen grab utilities, such as Command-Shift-3 (or 4), or use the Grab function found in Preview.

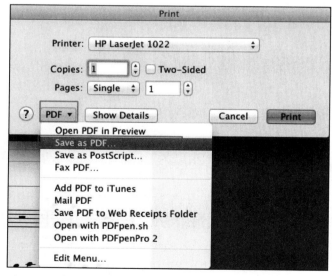

Figure 17.18 Saving a score as a PDF.

18 Layout Techniques for Parts

After preparing the full score, you can prepare the parts. Although you can certainly do so in the same project, as I have said before, I think it wiser to do so in a separate project.

1. Save the project under another name, such as **1m1-parts**.
2. Change the link in the Score Editor to the Content link (yellow link icon).
3. Unlock/relock the screenset.
4. Make sure Page Setup is letter size (if you are printing on 8.5 × 11" paper).

I choose my first part, the flute, and it appears as you see in Figure 18.1.

Much of what I will now change is totally subjective aesthetically. In my full score, I want the bar numbers centered, above the measure, and circled. I also want to see the long name at the beginning of the first line and short names on the subsequent lines. This is not what I want for parts, so I return to the Numbers and Names settings under Layout in the Score Window. See Figure 18.2. In Figure 18.3, you can see my settings for the full score.

Time to start making some changes.

1. In the Bar Numbers area, change Horizontal Position to At Bar Line.
2. Change Vertical Position to –1 so that the bar numbers are visible below the staff.
3. Because I only need the players to see the first bar number of each line, change Step to 0.
4. Check Follow Staff Size so that in smaller staff styles the bar number display will adjust to better suit its size.
5. Click the Choose button next to Font; set it to an uncircled font.
6. In the Instrument Names area, change Other Staffs to No Names. The settings now appear as you see in Figure 18.4; in Figure 18.5 you can see how the flute part looks with the changes.

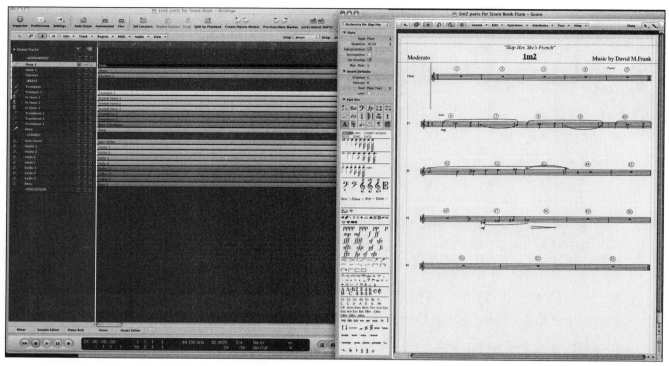

Figure 18.1 My 1m2 screenset for Parts prep.

Now you can actually make this into a part a flautist might want to read. Once again, many of my choices will be subjective and based on my experience. You or your friendly neighborhood flautist might disagree with some of them. The first thing I like to do is save this part as an individual Score Set to make returning to whatever formatting I do easier.

1. Choose Layout > Create Score Set from Selection, as shown in Figure 18.6. It creates a score set named *Flute 1.

2. Double-click the score set and change its name to **Flute** (because there is only one in this orchestra). See Figure 18.7. Already it is looking better, but there is too much space between the lines.

3. Double-click the Flute staff style to open it. The upper and lower Space settings default to 128 and 72. Double-click on 128 and type an educated guess. I type in 74 for this example. Double-click the 72 and type in **50**. See Figure 18.8.

4. Change Size to 9 so that the size is a litter bigger than the default of 8. As you can see in Figure 18.9, the part is starting to look pretty good. However, I see a few issues that I want to correct via the Layout tool.

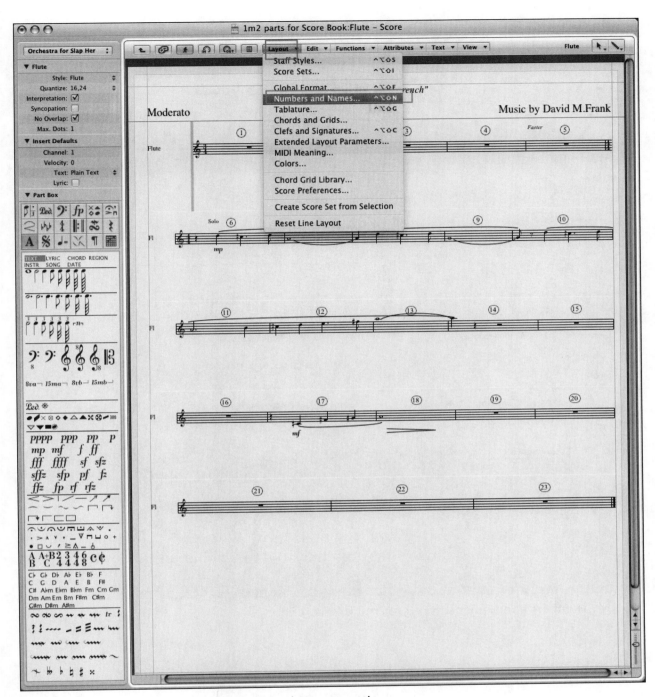

Figure 18.2 Returning to the Numbers and Names settings.

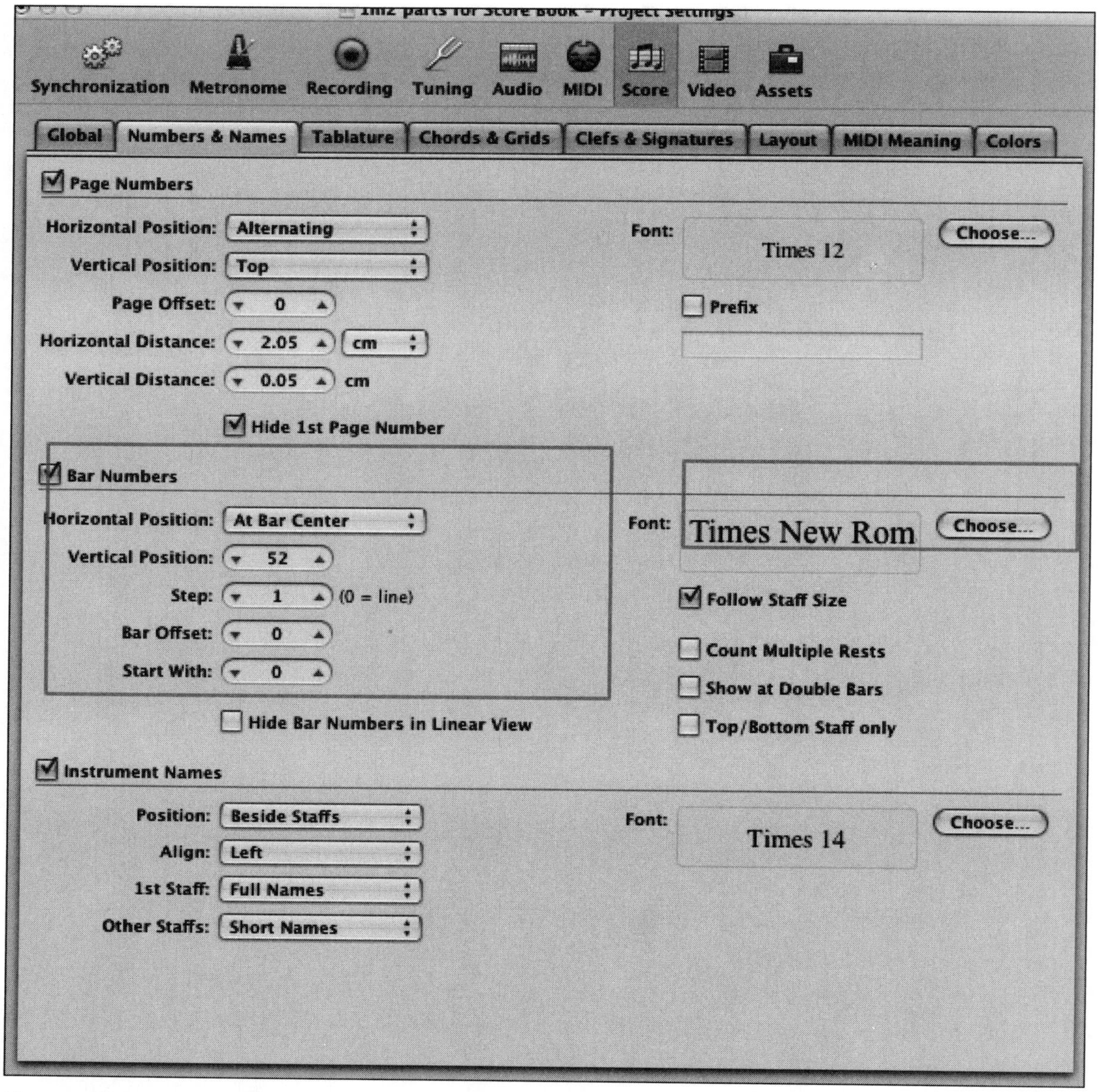

Figure 18.3 My Numbers and Names settings for the full score.

5. Change the Command tool to the Layout tool; see Figure 18.10. The tempo directions *Faster* and *Slower* are too high (see Figure 18.11). Holding down the Command tool, drag them down to where you deem appropriate.

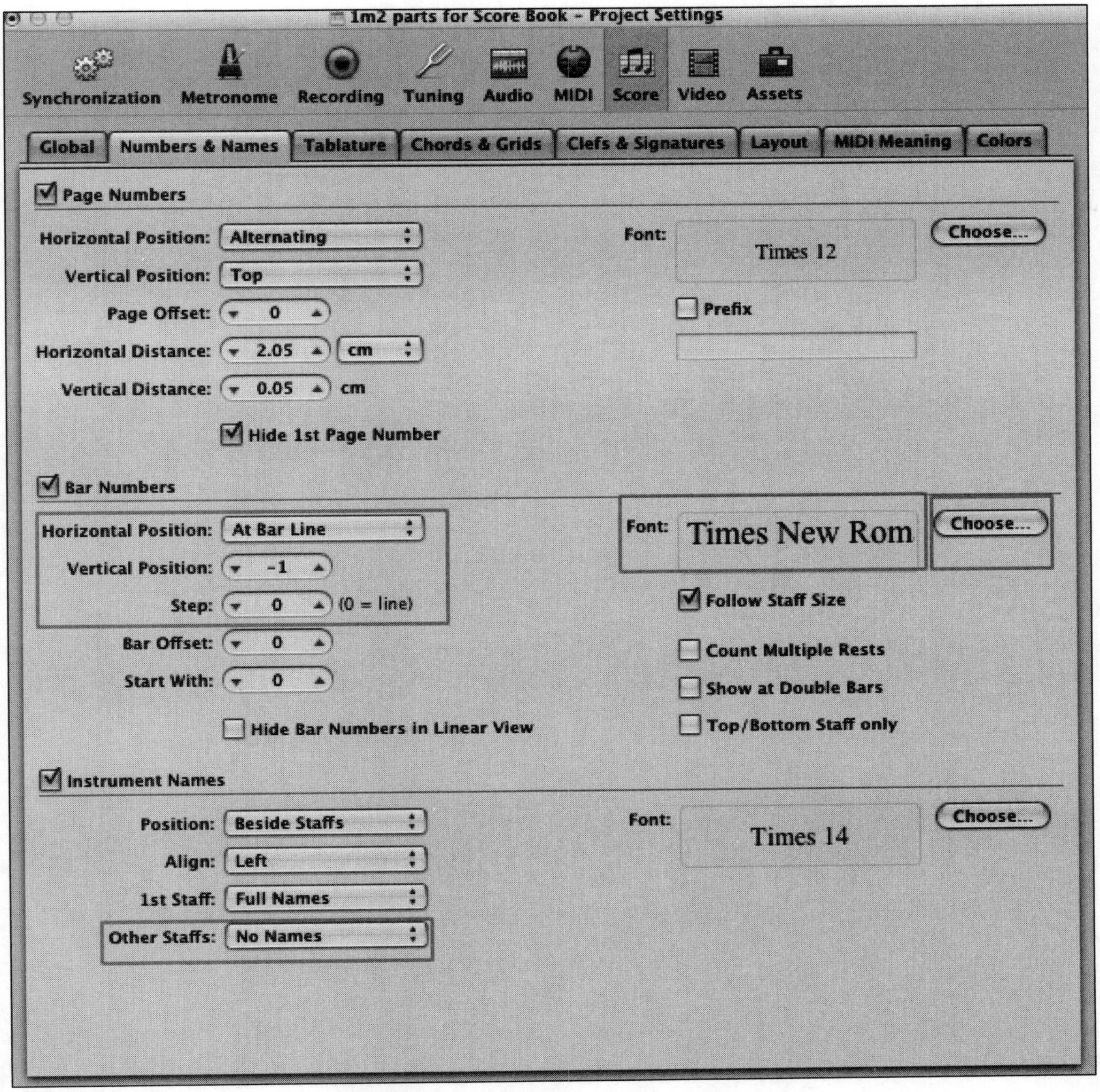

Figure 18.4 My Numbers and Names settings for the parts.

6. If you have not assigned a key command to Paste Multiple, do so now. I use Shift-Option-Command-V. Bar 5 has a tempo direction of Faster and bar 17 has one of Slower. On the full score, I only needed to look to the top, but I need it on every part. For this task you need the Paste Multiple key command.

7. Shift-select the two tempo instructions and press Command-C to copy.

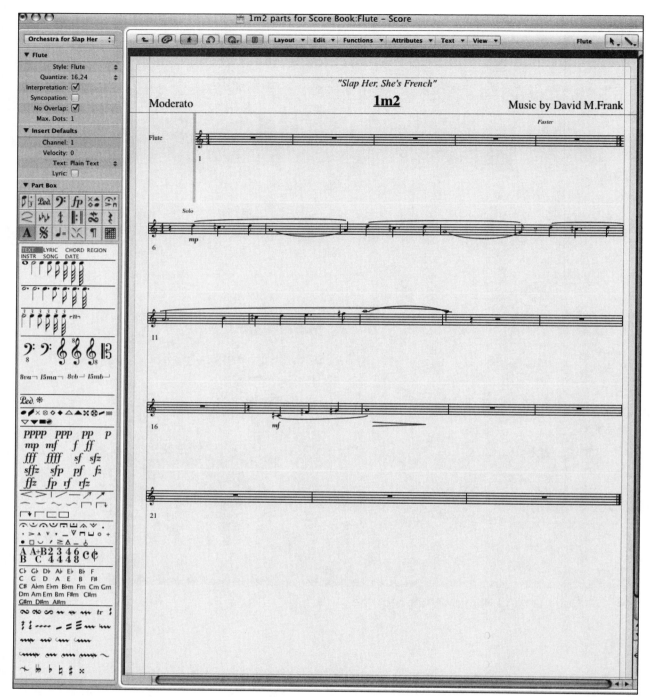

Figure 18.5 The flute part after the Name and Numbers settings changes.

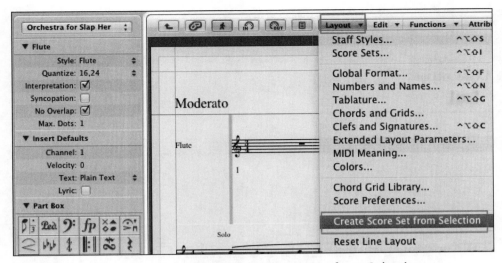

Figure 18.6 Choosing the option Create Score Set from Selection.

8. Return to the score set you created for the full orchestra and change the link to the Same Level (violet) link.

9. Press Command-A to select all, then Shift-select the flute part so it is the only *unselected* part. See Figure 18.12.

10. Move the playhead to where the first tempo instruction enters. (Use the Go To Position key command if you have one assigned.) The first tempo instruction enters at bar 5 in this example. Press the Paste Multiple key command, and voilà—they appear on every part.

11. Re-save the project. I usually choose a different version number by this point.

Whew! Consider it a bullet dodged. Had you entered it on all the parts first and then done the full score, you would have to delete the directions on every part in the score except for the flute, which is perhaps another good argument for doing the score first.

Now I return to my Flute score set and turn the link back to Show Content (yellow) by pressing the number for my locked screenset.

If this were a long cue, I would definitely want to insert some multi-rests. This is a shorter cue, but let's do it anyway.

1. Select the multi-rest symbol in the Part Box and drag it to bar 1. It inserts a five-bar multi-rest. See Figure 18.13. There is one problem: The tempo direction Faster now appears at bar 6 instead of bar 5.

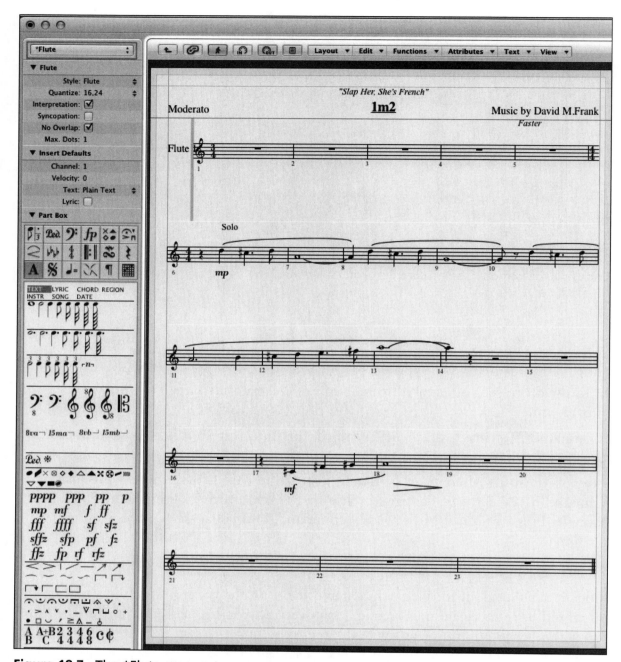

Figure 18.7 The *Flute score set.

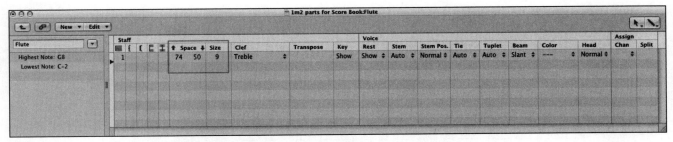

Figure 18.8 Changing the spacing and staff size in the Flute score set.

Figure 18.9 The flute part is starting to look good.

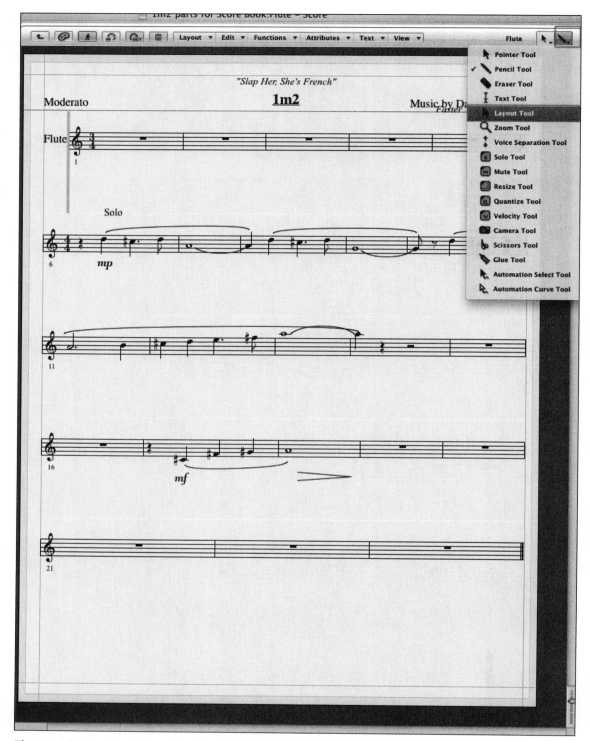

Figure 18.10 Changing the Command tool to the Layout tool.

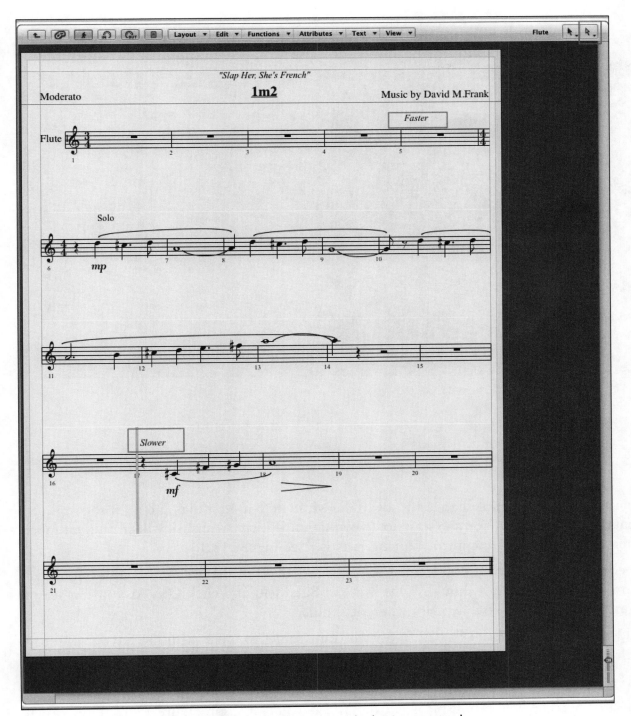

Figure 18.11 Repositioning the tempo directions with the Layout tool.

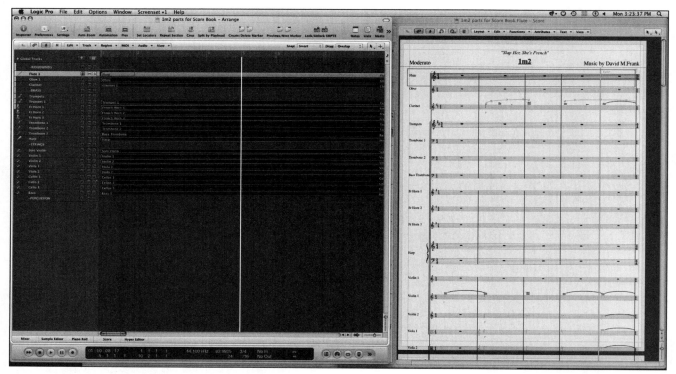

Figure 18.12 Unselecting the flute part.

2. Double-click the multiple bar rest to open the Multiple Bar Rest dialog box. It shows Auto Length as the default. (You can set it not to count multi-rests, but since it will be right far more often than wrong, I recommend leaving it as is.) See Figure 18.14.

3. Uncheck Auto Length. If you leave it selected, any text you have entered will no longer seem to appear where it should. Type **4** in the Bars field and click OK. As you can see in Figure 18.15, Faster now appears where it should.

4. Add another multi-rest at bar 22. Now it is time to get to work with the Layout tool to make it look a little better.

5. Press the Command key to make the Pointer tool become the Layout tool.

6. Select bar 6. The help tab displays Move Bars, as you can see in Figure 18.16. Drag down to the next line to make it look better.

7. Do the same with bar 15. Now I really like the formatting.

After some final tweaking to the slurs horizontally and vertically and making a little less space between lines (see Figure 18.17), I deem the part ready to print and hand to my flautist.

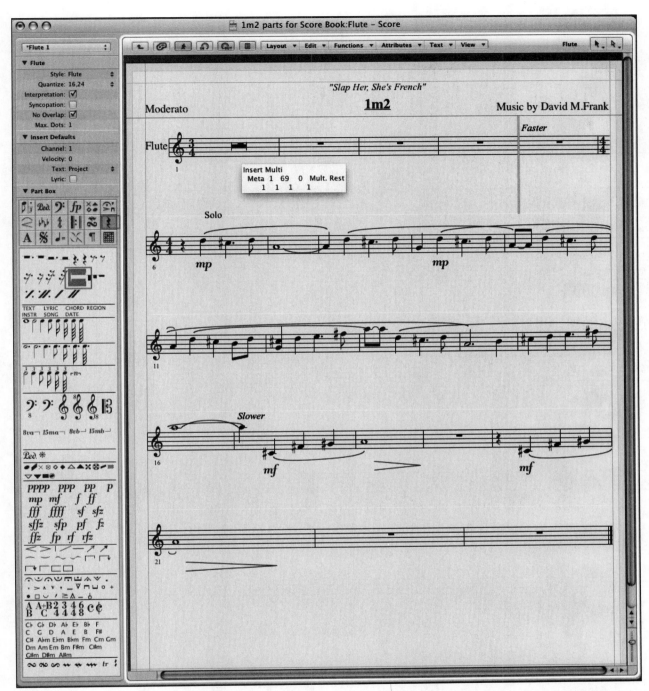

Figure 18.13 The multi-rest is inserted but makes the positioning of the tempo direction incorrect.

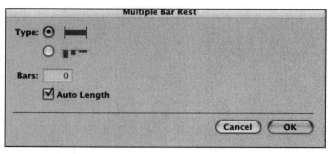

Figure 18.14 The Multiple Bar Rest dialog box.

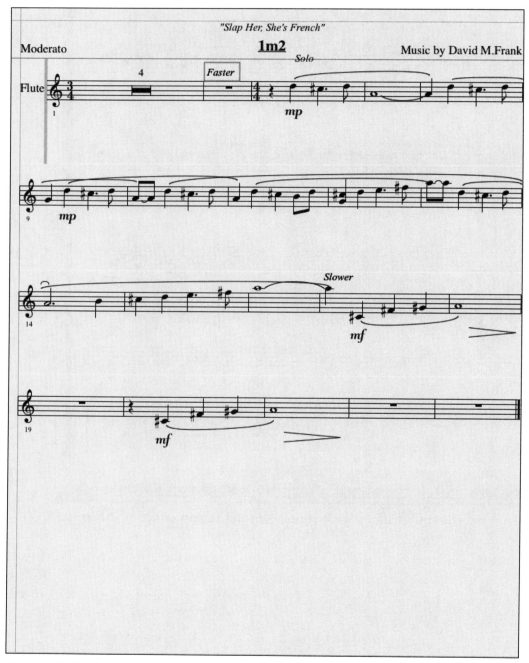

Figure 18.15 The four-bar multi-rest with Faster at bar 5.

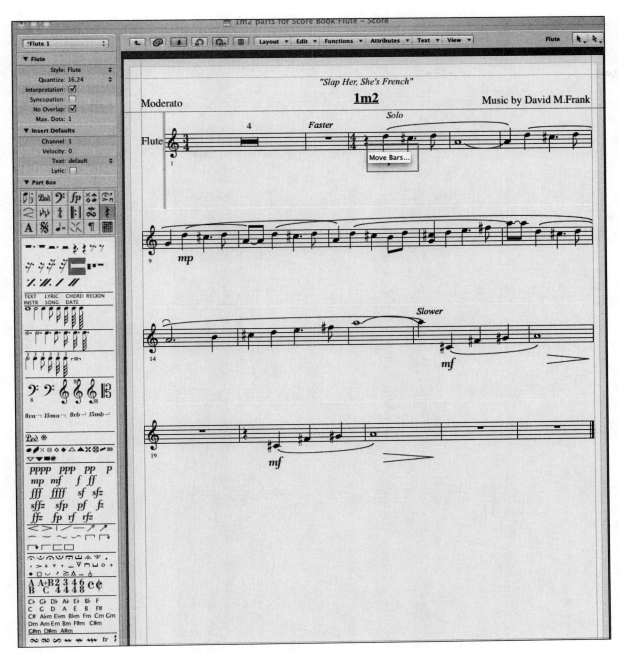

Figure 18.16   Moving bars with the Layout tool.

Now I return to the Orchestra score set, choose the next track in the Arrange Window's Track List (in this case, oboe), and choose Create Score Set from Selection. I am ready to do the same things for the oboe part that I did for the flute part, knowing that whatever formatting I do to the oboe part will not affect the flute part. Because I already created and assigned the desired staff styles to the parts

Figure 18.17 The flute part is ready to print.

when I prepared the full score, there will be less work to do now. I can prepare all my parts this way with confidence, even though the &*$^ line breaks and page breaks do not work as they should. This may seem like a laborious process, but you will be pleasantly surprised at how fast you can get at doing it.

19 Preparing Chord Charts for Sessions

This may be the most important tutorial for Logic users who are songwriters and arrangers (rather than film composers or orchestrators). Typically, a chord chart is composed of a part for a musician accompanying a soloist or vocalist. Sometimes the parts are composed of nothing more than chord symbols and slashes to show the beats. This is generally the case with simple rock, pop, or country songs. The advantage is that you only need to prepare one chart that can be handed out to the pianist, guitarist, bassist, and even the drummer. Everyone will have a basic guide for what they are going to play, with guidance from the writer, arranger, or producer. The disadvantage is that you are not giving the player much information about what you want him to play. This, of course, can work to a songwriter's advantage when she has not determined what she wants the players to play, except for the chords.

Chord charts for each player are more commonly used. Chord charts include basic note or rhythmic figures in measures that begin an intro, verse, chorus, bridge, and so on, followed by measures with the chords and rhythmic slashes. This gives the player some guidance to the basic approach yet leaves them freedom to use their creativity to play an interesting part that the composer may not have conceived of. Obviously, doing so more thoroughly takes more time, but unless you are under the gun, it is well worth the effort. It gives the players a message about your level of commitment.

You may be preparing this from scratch, or perhaps you have already played in some MIDI information on a Software Instrument track. In Figure 19.1, you can see that I am starting from scratch with a blank region. I have, however, already entered all my header info and created a boxed text style for traditional rehearsal letters, which I will copy to each part. I recommend getting in the habit of doing this if you are not already. Your sessions will go much more smoothly.

In Tutorial 14, I explain how to work with chord symbols. Entering the chord symbols is what you do first.

1. Enter the chord symbols. See Figure 19.2.

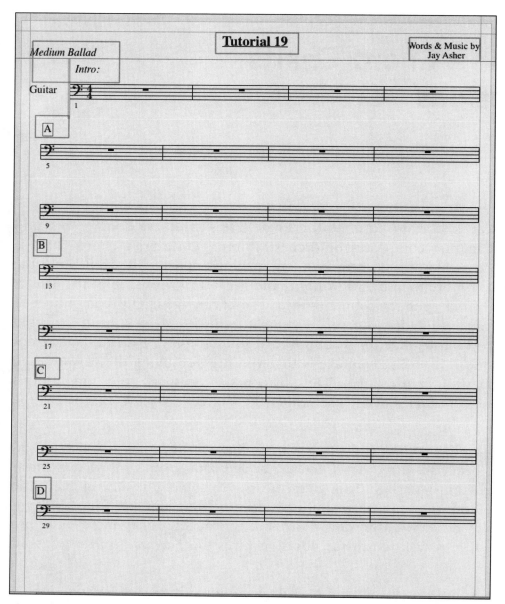

Figure 19.1 A blank region with header info and rehearsal letters.

2. You want the guitar to do an 8th note strum in the Intro section. Enter single notes in the first measure in the middle of the staff, like in Figure 19.3. Change the note head. (You do not want these specific pitches, only chords played with this rhythm.)

Figure 19.2 The chord symbols entered.

3.   Go to the note head group in the Part Box; click the slash (the second symbol in the first line). With all the notes selected, drag the note head symbol onto the first note. See Figure 19.4.

4.   Repeat the process for any measure where you want the guitar to play a different rhythm. In Figure 19.5, I have done precisely that.

Figure 19.3   The desired rhythm entered with single notes.

Entering Licks

Now you are ready to enter any licks you need. I have one in mind to transition from the verse to the choruses over the D7 chord.

1.   Enter the lick in bar 12 and copy it to bar 28. See Figure 19.6. Many songwriters/arrangers do not add traditional dynamics on pop, rock, and country songs, but any

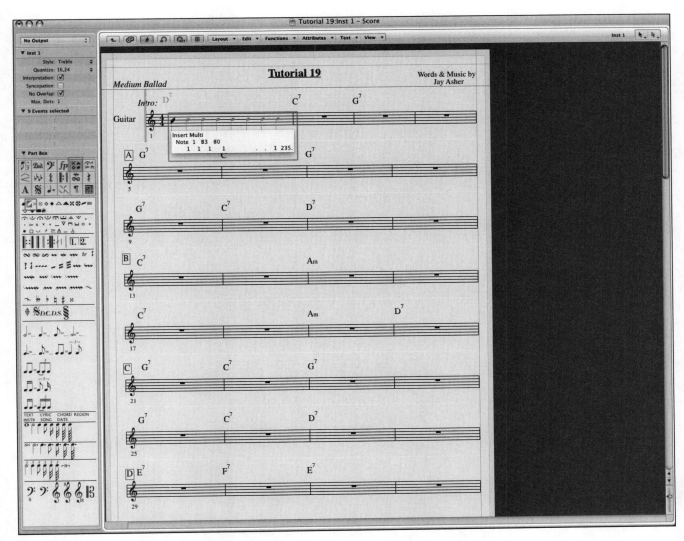

Figure 19.4 Changing the note heads.

clarification you add will help the session go more smoothly. In Figure 19.7 you can see added dynamics.

This is shaping up nicely. The guitarist now has all the specific information he needs. It is time to fill in, which involves creating and using a staff style that displays slashes instead of rests.

2. Using the method shown in Tutorial 18, duplicate the Treble staff style. See Figure 19.8.

Figure 19.5 All the rhythmic patterns have been entered.

3. Double-click the Treble*copied staff style. In the Voice section for Rest, change the setting to Slash (as shown in Figure 19.9). In Figure 19.10, you can see the result.

4. The slashes fill in every beat where there are no MIDI notes. What if you want a rest preceded by an accented chord? Drag/pencil them in. Figure 19.11 shows exactly that in bar 20. This puppy is ready to print!

Figure 19.6 Adding some licks for the guitar.

Using Repeat Signs

Rather than starting from scratch, you may wish to modify an existing MIDI part. In Figure 19.12, I played in a bass part and copied all the dynamics and rehearsal letters from the guitar part. If you want to use a staff style with slashes, you have to select and delete a lot of notes. That is

Figure 19.7 Adding dynamics.

Figure 19.8 Duplicating the Treble staff style.

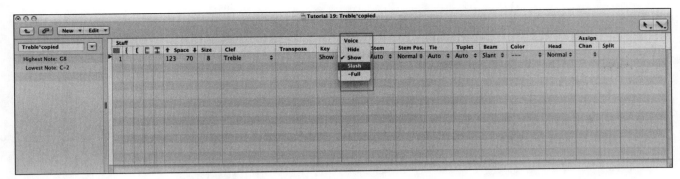

Figure 19.9 Changing the Rest setting to Slash.

Figure 19.10 Filling in the guitar part with slashes.

Figure 19.11 Adding a user rest preceded by an accented note.

certainly not a big deal, but here is another method using repeat signs. In Figure 19.13, I have cho-sen the Part Box's rest group—specifically, the repeat symbol.

Now simply choose the Pencil tool and pencil the symbol anywhere into each measure where the rhythmic pattern is repeated. See Figure 19.14. As a pianist, in many cases I prefer this to reading slashes, but either is just fine for most pop/rock/country musicians.

Figure 19.12   A MIDI bass part.

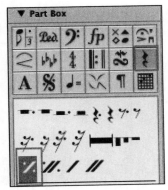

Figure 19.13   Selecting the repeat symbol.

Figure 19.14 The bass part with repeat symbols.

20 Preparing Lead Sheets

This tutorial not only provides methods for creating a range of lead sheets (from very basic to more complex) but also reviews a few key subjects. My suspicion is that more of you will use Logic Pro's Score Editor for creating chord charts and lead sheets than anything else.

A *lead sheet* commonly refers to a score with a part or parts for melodic soloists or singers with lyrics, plus a part for an accompanist (usually a pianist). Although this short tutorial mostly consists of completing tasks I covered in earlier tutorials, this topic is more complex than preparing chord charts, for several reasons.

The main reason it's more complex has to do with the nature of the lead sheet's purpose. It also relates to the accompanist's training and habits. If the singer is pop or country, for instance, the pianist is likely to be most comfortable with the approach explained in Tutorial 19. Indeed, the singer may have only rudimentary (or no) skills with reading traditional two-stave piano notation. Others, particularly in musical theater, may sight read the heck out of traditional two-stave piano notation but have no clue about how to play from the kind of chord charts explored in Tutorial 19. Still others will want to see the traditional two-stave piano notation plus chord symbols so they can use both to help rehearse singers. On the other hand, the only thing that may be required is a Real Book style part with the melody, chord changes, and lyrics. You absolutely need to know what the players require in their lead sheet.

In Figure 20.1, you can see a Real Book style lead sheet, which might be just fine for many purposes.

Figure 20.2 shows a more sophisticated lead sheet that has a vocal melody with lyrics, a piano part with chords and rhythmic features, and a staff style with slashes in a score set that I named Piano/Vocal (scaled to 70%), as that is how it is commonly referred to. See the Piano/Vocal score set in Figure 20.3. These were very easy to create and you can do so quickly with Logic Pro's Score Editor.

As is typical in the musical theater world, pianists expect to see two-stave piano parts without chord symbols and the vocal parts are expected to be precise. (If you take on this kind of job,

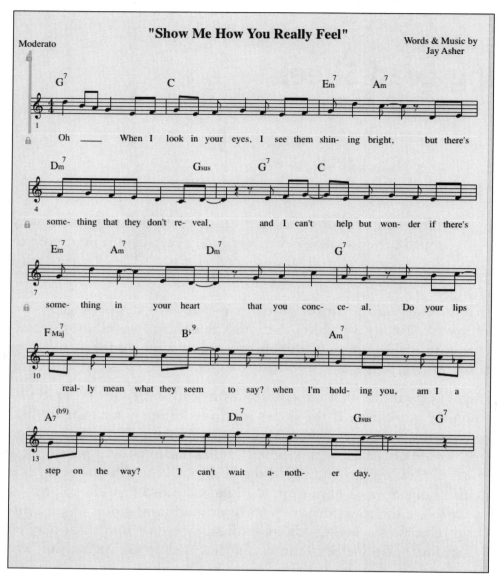

Figure 20.1 A Real Book style lead sheet.

be prepared for some hard work and make sure you are paid well.) Figure 20.4 shows a section of a lead sheet for a duet with piano accompaniment, "My Love For You."

The techniques I used are discussed throughout this book, but let me give you an idea of what I needed to do to get it to this state (and provide a refresher course).

- First I created the vocal parts that would be used as parts, part of the full score, and the lead sheet. The vocal parts feature contemporary rhythms. When syncopation was enabled, some rhythmic figures looked correct while others looked incorrect. When syncopation was disabled, some rhythmic figures looked correct while others looked incorrect. Ultimately, I

Figure 20.2   A more sophisticated lead sheet.

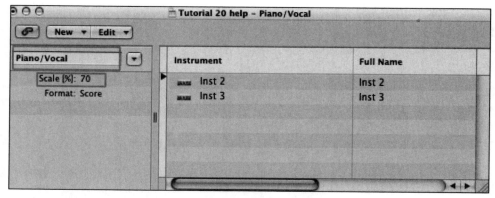

Figure 20.3   The Piano/Vocal score set scaled to 70%.

Figure 20.4   The lead sheet for "My Love For You."

did not enable syncopation. Instead, I highlighted the figures I wanted displayed as syncopated, and as previously explained, I forced syncopation for those notes. I made that setting under the Attributes menu. See Figure 20.5.

- The same issue existed for Interpretation. I enabled it in the Display Parameters Box. I defeated it on the notes where it did not work, again under the Attributes menu. See Figure 20.6.

- Regarding the vocal parts: Because lyrics are not part of the MIDI specs and are proprietary to each application, I had to enter the lyrics for the two singers. I explain that in Tutorial 8.

Figure 20.5   Forcing syncopation.

Figure 20.6   Defeating Interpretation.

Figure 20.7 The piano part with the generic Piano staff style.

With the vocal parts completed, it was time to turn to the piano part. As with many fine orchestrations for musical theater, it is not uncommon for the piano not to play throughout the entire song. This meant that I had to create sections of the part from other instruments in the orchestra that were playing harmonic accompaniment—usually the string section. While doing so is not difficult, it IS time consuming. There were many places in the piano part where within the same staff, there were held notes and moving lines. This, of course, means using the Polyphonic staff style, as discussed in Tutorial 4.

In Figure 20.7, you can see how the part would look with the generic Piano staff style. This is clearly unacceptable as there are notes displayed in each hand that clearly belong to the other

Figure 20.8   The piano part with the Piano 1/3,4 Polyphonic staff style.

hand. Figure 20.8, however, shows the default Piano 1/3,4 Polyphonic staff style with proper MIDI channel assignment to allocate the notes. The notes appear in the correct staff and the piano part looks very good indeed. Notice the various MIDI channels that I used to accomplish this look in the piano region's Event List. See Figure 20.9.

| Event | Marker | Tempo | Signature |

Edit ▾   Functions ▾   View ▾

Filter   Create   off (3840)   Q

| Notes | Progr. Change | Pitch Bend | Controller |
| Chnl Pressure | Poly Pressure | Syst. Exclusive | Additional Info |

Position				Status	Ch	Num	Val	Length/Info			
1	1	1	1	Meta	1	62	4	Score Symbol			
1	1	1	1	Note	1	E3	74	.	2	0	18
1	1	1	1	Note	1	G3	84	.	3	3	194
1	1	1	1	Note	3	C2	84	.	2	0	30
1	1	1	1	Note	3	G2	84	.	2	0	30
1	1	1	57	Note	4	D4	107	.	.	3	180
1	1	4	232	Note	4	C4	100	.	1	0	0
1	2	4	205	Note	4	B3	93	.	1	0	48
1	3	1	1	Note	1	C3	86	1	1	3	198
1	3	1	1	Note	1	E3	86	1	1	3	198
1	3	1	1	Note	3	A1	84	.	1	3	192
1	3	1	1	Note	3	E2	84	.	1	3	192
1	3	4	201	Note	4	A3	77	.	1	0	5
1	4	4	180	Note	4	G3	105	.	1	0	120
2	1	1	1	Note	1	F2	82	1	2	0	82
2	1	1	1	Note	1	C3	82	1	2	0	82
2	1	1	1	Note	3	D1	79	.	1	3	146
2	1	1	1	Note	3	D2	79	.	1	3	146
2	2	1	18	Note	4	F3	100	.	.	3	220
2	2	4	191	Note	1	E3	115	.	2	0	96
2	3	1	1	Note	1	C3	82	1	2	0	82
2	3	1	1	Note	3	G1	77	1	0	0	48
2	3	1	1	Note	3	F2	82	1	2	0	82
3	1	1	1	Note	1	B2	82	1	0	0	74
3	1	1	9	Note	1	D3	107	1	0	0	105
4	1	1	1	Note	1	G2	51	.	.	2	192
4	1	1	1	Note	1	D3	51	.	.	2	228
4	1	1	1	Note	3	C1	58	.	3	2	82
4	2	1	1	Note	1	G2	49	.	.	2	144
4	2	1	1	Note	1	C3	55	.	.	2	150
4	3	1	1	Note	1	G2	47	.	.	2	56
4	3	1	1	Note	1	B2	52	.	.	2	90
4	4	1	1	Note	1	G2	49	.	.	1	110
4	4	1	1	Note	1	C3	57	.	.	1	156
5	1	1	1	Note	1	A2	49	.	.	2	54
5	1	1	1	Note	1	E3	51	.	.	2	80
5	1	1	1	Note	3	F1	45	.	3	3	114
5	2	1	1	Note	1	A2	41	.	.	2	108
5	2	1	1	Note	1	D3	39	.	.	2	122
5	3	1	1	Note	1	A2	36	.	.	2	14
5	3	1	1	Note	1	C3	39	.	.	2	28
5	4	1	1	Note	1	A2	61	.	.	1	72
5	4	1	1	Note	1	D3	57	.	.	1	64
6	1	1	1	Note	1	G2	53	.	.	2	56
6	1	1	1	Note	1	D3	51	.	.	2	116
6	1	1	1	Note	3	C1	60	.	3	2	188

Figure 20.9 The necessary MIDI channel assignments performed in the piano region for proper display with the Piano 1/3,4 Polyphonic staff style.

Because the piano part was not going to be used outside of the lead sheet, I saved the project under a separate name for the lead sheet. Alternatively, I could have kept it as a track in the full score version and simply hid the track later. But, hey, it's only a little hard-drive space, right?

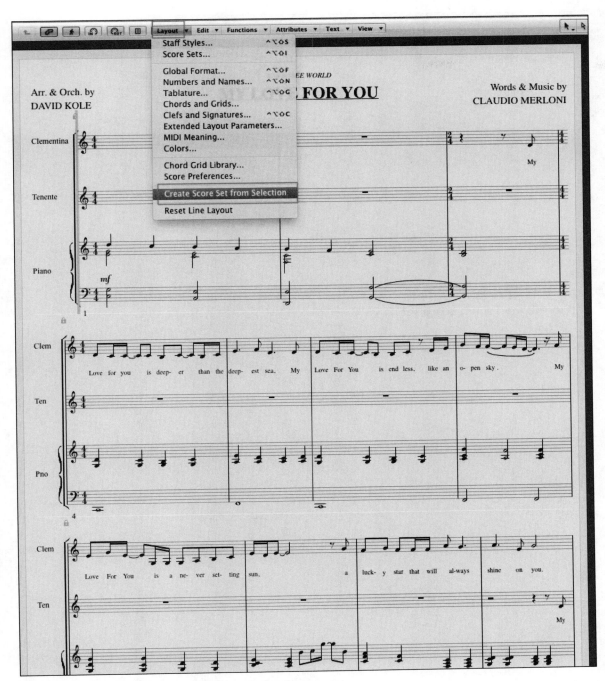

Figure 20.10   Create Score Set from Selection.

Now it was a matter of selecting the three regions and choosing Layout > Create Score Set from Selection, as shown in Figure 20.10. I double-clicked the score set to scale it to 73%, as shown in Figure 20.11.

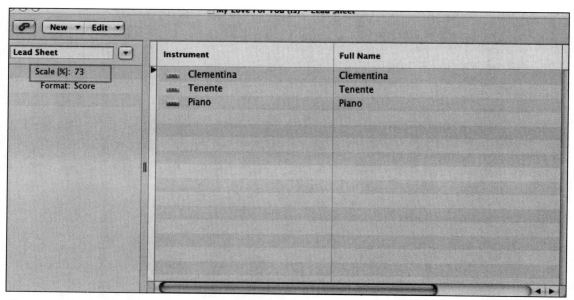

Figure 20.11 Scaling the lead sheet score set to 73%.

21 Preparing Master Rhythm Charts

A master rhythm chart is one designed for song arrangements for all the rhythm section players to play from (duh!). Once again, the charts come in different flavors, but a properly written one has at least the following: chords, main rhythms, important licks, dynamics, and instructions for tempo. They may also include lyrical cues.

Traditional master rhythm charts are written on two or three staves (or as many as needed in different parts of the song). Because it is much easier to go from two to three to four writing on score paper, I tend to pick one and make it work. In this case, I use three staves. In Figure 21.1, you can see the individual parts that you are going to assemble. In most cases, you would simply do one from scratch, but for demonstration purposes, you will work with this.

1. My personal preference for the copying and pasting that I will need to do now is to work in Linear View rather than Page View, so under the View menu I make the change by unchecking Page View. See Figure 21.2.

   Now you want to get rid of material that you do not need, and paste from other tracks into the piano track. Keep the piano riff in the right hand at the beginning.

2. Double-click the Piano staff style that is assigned to the piano region. Change Split to B2 and Rest to Show. See Figure 21.3.

3. Select the left-hand notes and press Delete. You should see what appears in Figure 21.4.

4. Now open either the Event List or an Event Float. I do the latter in Figure 21.5. You need what the bass is playing for the first five bars, so rubberband over the notes with your mouse to select them. In the Event Float, change their MIDI channel assignment to 3 so that will appear in the left hand of your piano region. See Figure 21.6.

5. Press Command-C, choose the piano region (making sure that the playhead is at bar 1), and press Command-V.

6. Continue this process until any notes or rhythmic figures you deem necessary for the bass are entered into the piano region. Although it is not essential, you might choose the remaining regions and create a score set. I have done that many times before in this book. That way you are no longer viewing the bass part.

Figure 21.1 My song as it presently appears.

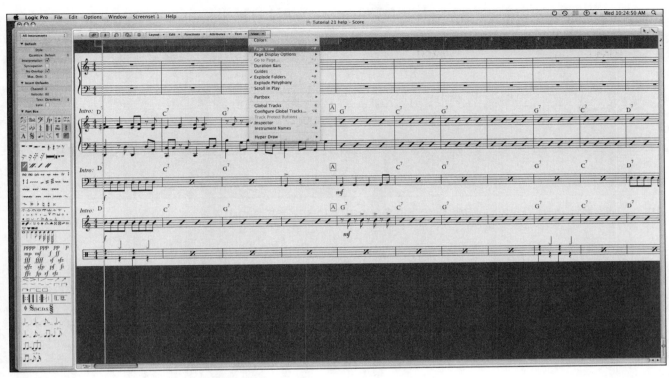

Figure 21.2 Changing to Linear View.

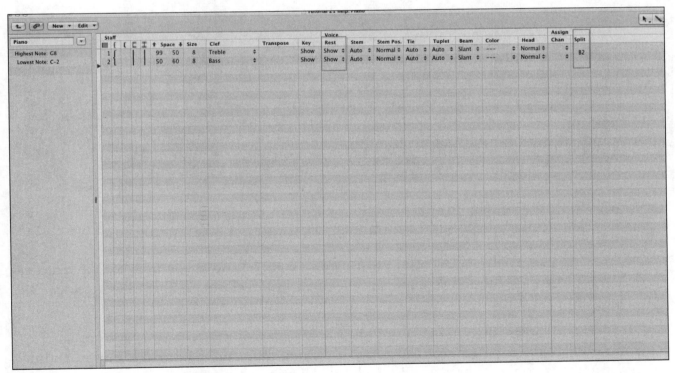

Figure 21.3 Altering the Piano staff style.

Figure 21.4 The piano region after deleting the notes in the left hand.

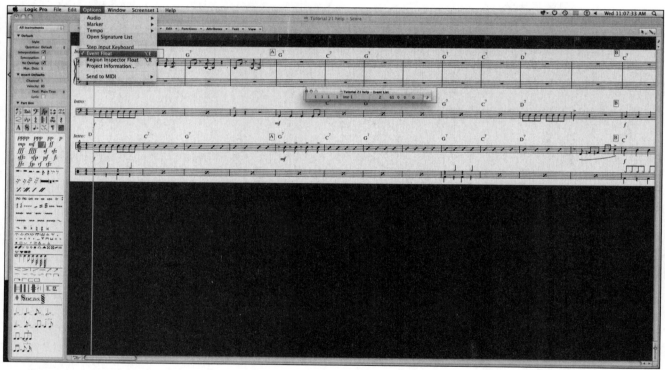

Figure 21.5 The Event Float.

7. Clarify what the players are seeing by using the same text style you used for the rehearsal letters. Enter the instruments' names in the appropriate places directly into the score. See Figure 21.7.

It is time to integrate the guitar using the same methodology. However, you see an opportunity at the beginning. The guitar is playing the same rhythm as the bass, and the root notes are obvious because of the chord changes.

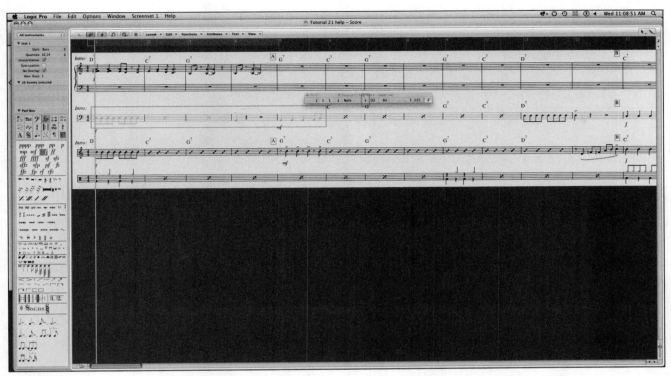

Figure 21.6 Changing the MIDI channel assignments of the bass notes in the Event Float.

Figure 21.7 Using text for clarification.

8. Change the note heads of the bass notes in bars 1 and 4. They should look like those of the guitar part.

9. Double-click the text that reads *Bass* and change it to Bass & Guitar. See Figure 21.8.

Figure 21.8 Updating the text and note head display.

10. That was easy. Now keep copying and pasting the essential material from the guitar. When that is complete, create a new score set without the guitar. Now return to Page View, which is shown in Figure 21.9.

Figure 21.9 The newer and smaller score set.

You are in the home stretch. If you were hand-writing on score paper, you would simply write in the drum rhythms where they change (between the two staffs, as shown in the first line of Figure 21.10).

Unfortunately, in Logic Pro's Score Editor, that involves manipulating a four-voice Polyphonic staff style. However, what you see in the bottom line is easily doable from your current point.

11. Under the Layout menu, choose Numbers and Names. Deselect Instrument Names. You don't need them.

12. All the manually created instrument names are the same size as the rehearsal letters. They both use the same text style, but here they look too big. Shift-select and scale them smaller (in this case –4, 0) with the Resize tool. See Figure 21.11. (I demonstrated this

Figure 21.10 A hand-written master rhythm chart.

Figure 21.11 Selecting the Resize tool.

method in Tutorial 6, where I talked about creating beamed grace notes.) In Figure 21.12, the instrument names' size looks better to me.

Time to do some tweaking in the #Drums staff style and the score set. What you do next is perhaps inconsistent with the hand-written example, but I like it.

13. Double-click the #Drums staff style. In the Clef settings, change the clef from Drum.5 (a five-line clef) to Drum.1 (a one-line clef). See Figure 21.13.

14. Double-click on the score set to open it and, in the second bracket column, draw all three staffs connected.

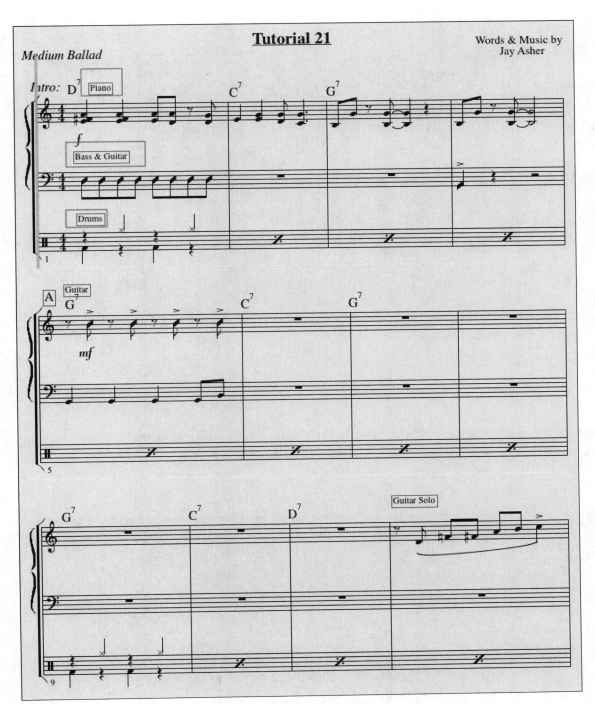

Figure 21.12 The instrument names look better smaller.

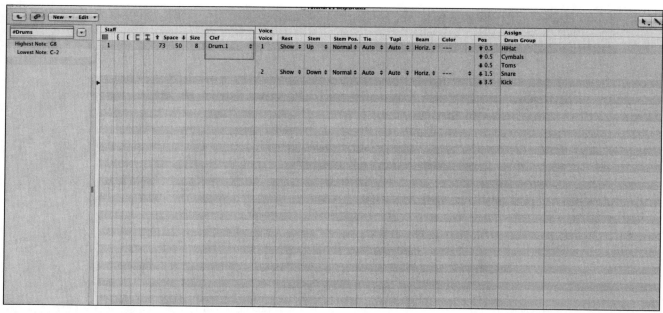

Figure 21.13 Changing the clef to Drum.1.

15. Eliminate any lines in the first, third, and fourth columns by dragging the line up until it disappears. Scale the score set to 72%, as shown in Figure 21.14.

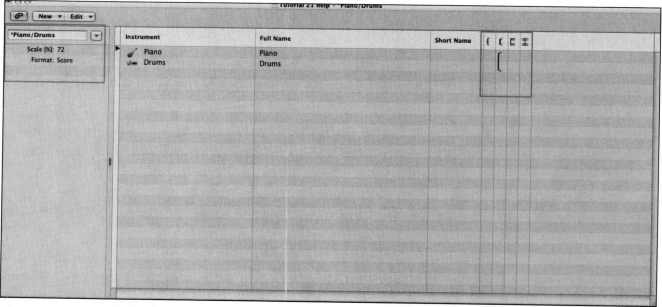

Figure 21.14 Score set scaled to 72%.

16.   Select the first chord change and press Shift-S (for Select Similar Events). With the Layout tool, position the chord changes between the staffs instead of above the top staff, as between the staffs is most common and easy to read in master rhythm charts.

All that remains now is repositioning things with the Layout tool. They should look best to your eye. Look at this nice master rhythm chart in Figure 21.15.

Figure 21.15   A completed master rhythm chart.

22 Things You May Never Need to Know...

This tutorial reveals techniques that appear infrequently for recording sessions. It also provides tips for fine-tuning the appearance of your parts and scores.

Codas

Codas and repeat signs most commonly occur in published music. Rarely have they occurred in recording sessions with which I have been involved. That said, codas and repeat signs can come in handy if you are recording a pop song. In that case there are fewer pages for the player to read from. In Figure 22.1, you can see a piano part for a rather basic bluesy ditty.

The first 16 bars should be repeated, but the second time around, I should jump directly to bar 17 and play until the end.

1. From the Part Box, insert the appropriate repeat signs at bar 1 and at the end of bar 16. The help tag says 17 1 1 1 for the repeat sign you are dragging to the end of bar 16. That is what you want. Repeat signs are global, which means they appear on every part in the project. Now add a double bar symbol at the end of the piece. See Figure 22.2.

2. Add coda symbols where the music jumps to the coda and the beginning of the coda itself. In Figure 22.3, they are correctly entered. (Generally, I use the Resize tool to make the latter symbol larger.) In the next step, you enter text to make perfectly clear where the music is going.

3. Generally, I like to box the word *Coda*. I created a text style for this in my template, as discussed in Tutorial 8. See Figure 22.4.

    Traditionally, the coda starts on a new line and with more space between the staffs. Some people like to indent it as well, but I do not.

4. Using the Scissors tool, split the region at bar 17—the beginning of the coda. Change the link to Same Level Link (violet) to make both regions visible.

5. Select the second region and duplicate the staff style (in this case, Treble). In Figure 22.5, the second region is assigned to the copied Treble staff style.

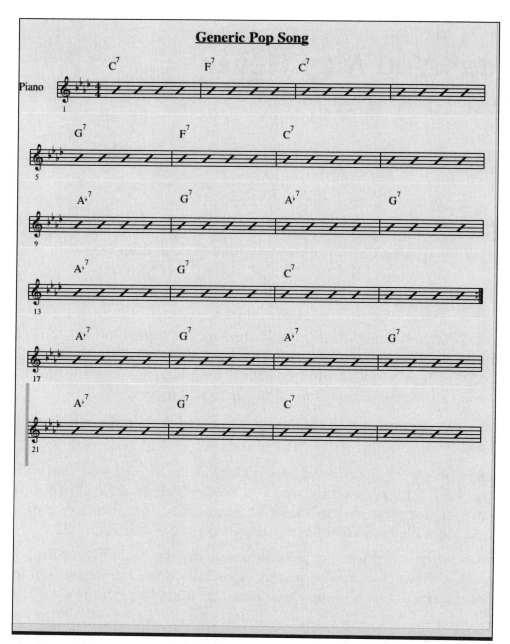

Figure 22.1 The piano part.

6. Click and hold on the clef at the beginning of the second region, and drag down to create more space. As you can see in Figure 22.6, there is too much space between the lines in the coda.

7. Cut the region at bar 21 and assign the newly created region to the original Treble staff style.

8. Select all the regions and perform Create Score Set From Selection. The part is looking the way you want it to with the coda. See Figure 22.7.

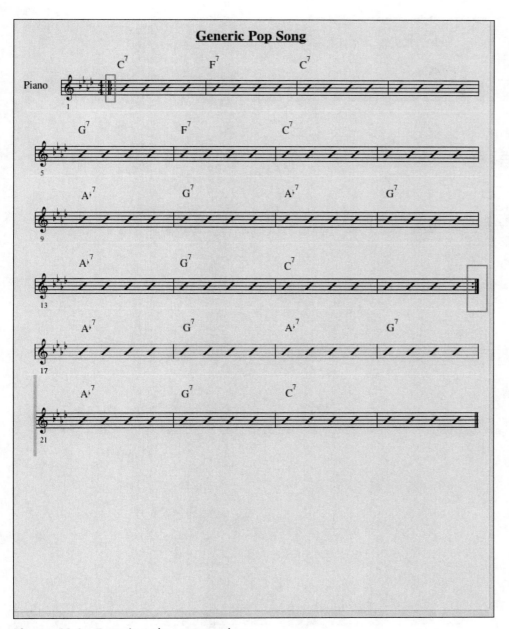

Figure 22.2 Entering the repeat signs.

Using the 8va/8vb Symbols

Figure 22.8 shows a violin part. Actually, most good violinists read those ledger lines just fine, but lesser musicians may not.

1. In the Part Box, in the Clefs group, select the 8ve up symbol. See Figure 22.9.

2. Drag it into the part, and it appears as you see in Figure 22.10. The Help tag may show that you are dragging the symbol to position 1 1 1 1, but if you place it a little higher, you can get it to align at 0 4 3 1, which is what you need.

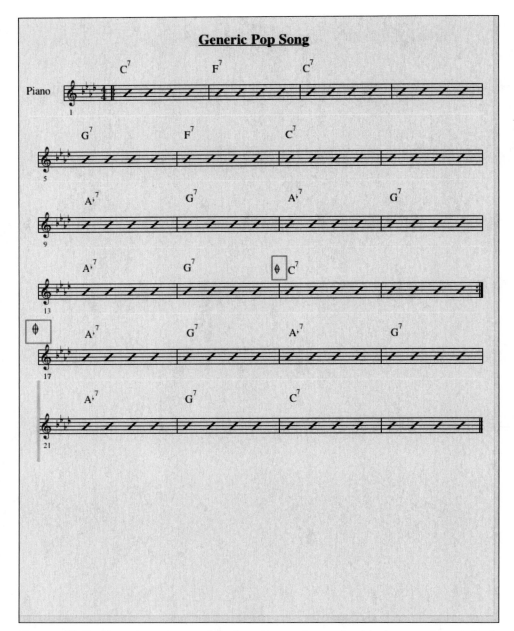

Figure 22.3 The piano part with the repeat signs, double bar at the region's end, and the coda symbols.

3. Notice that the notes already appear an octave lower over the notes that the symbol is over, but it is not over the duration of the entire part. Grab the right-hand corner and drag it to the desired duration, as shown in Figure 22.11.

4. In Figure 22.12, the symbol's placement is correct.

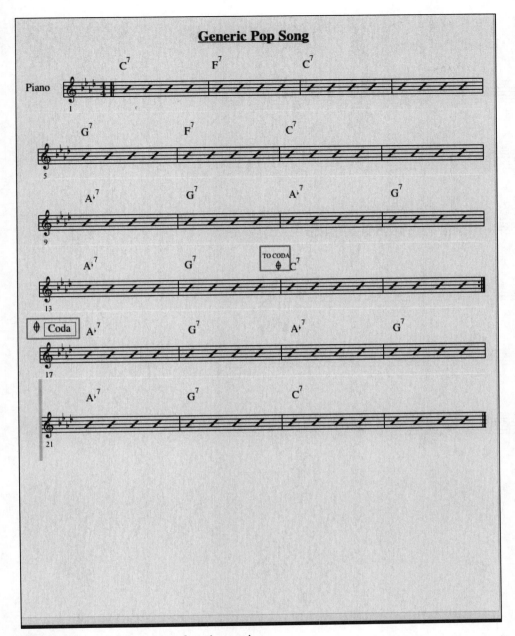

Figure 22.4 Adding text for the codas.

Fine-Tuning the Display of Symbols and Text in Parts and Scores

You can fine-tune symbol positions a number of ways—use the Layout tool to manually manipulate them by handles or select the symbols and adjust their horizontal and vertical position in the Event Parameter Box in the Inspector. But—particularly with slurs—this can mean unpredictable results.

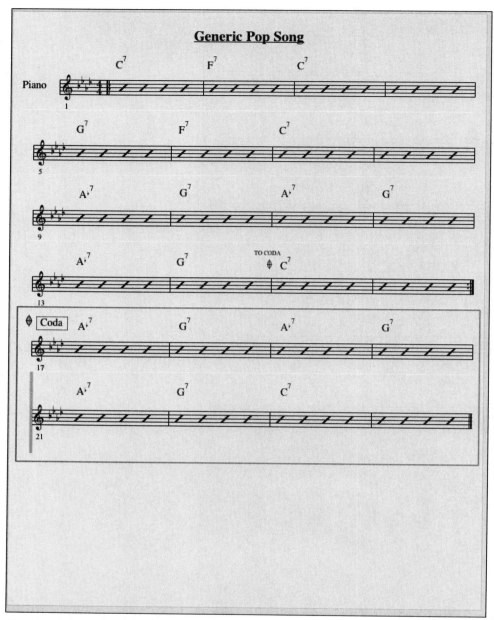

Figure 22.5 Reassigning the staff style for the second region.

As is frequently the case with Logic Pro, key commands that can be quite helpful. Some commands are pre-assigned and some you have to assign yourself. Let me call your attention to a few that are well worth your time. Figure 22.13 shows some that are not assigned. Align Horizontally and Align Vertically are my personal must-haves.

Tutorial 8 explored creating title, composer, and directions text for insertion into the header. In that tutorial, you dragged the TEXT, LYRIC, and CHORD words in the Part Box for insertion

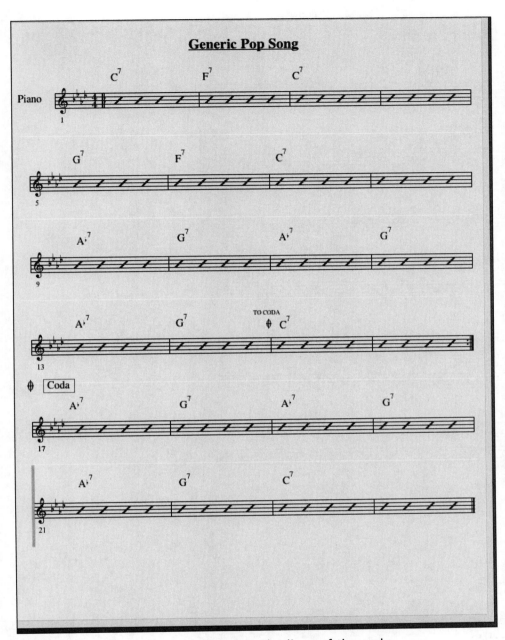

Figure 22.6   Too much space between the lines of the coda.

of those things into the score. However, you may want to explore other options—especially the Footer option. See Figure 22.14.

1. Figure 22.15 shows an unsuccessful attempt to drag the song title into the footer. It only inserts into *Bottom*.

2. In the Event Parameter Box, change Zone to Footer. Adjust Vertical Position, Horizontal Position, and Text Style to your taste. Leave Alignment centered. In Figure 22.16 you

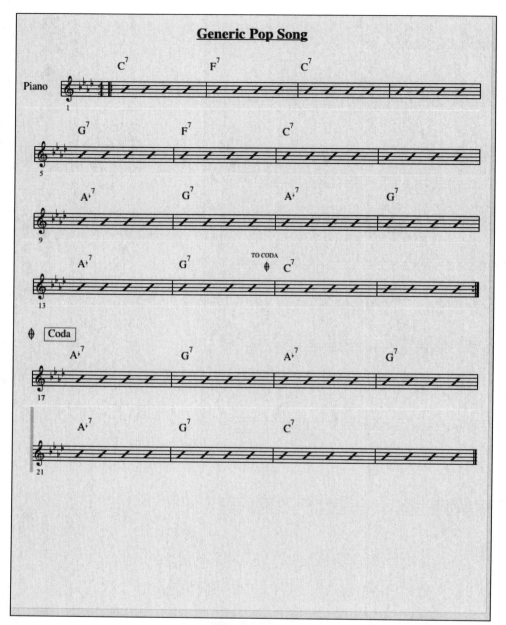

Figure 22.7 The coda looks correct.

Figure 22.8 The violin part.

Figure 22.9   The 8ve symbol in the Part Box.

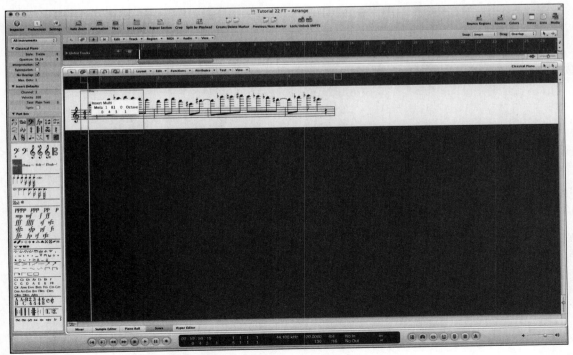

Figure 22.10   Adding the 8ve up symbol to the part.

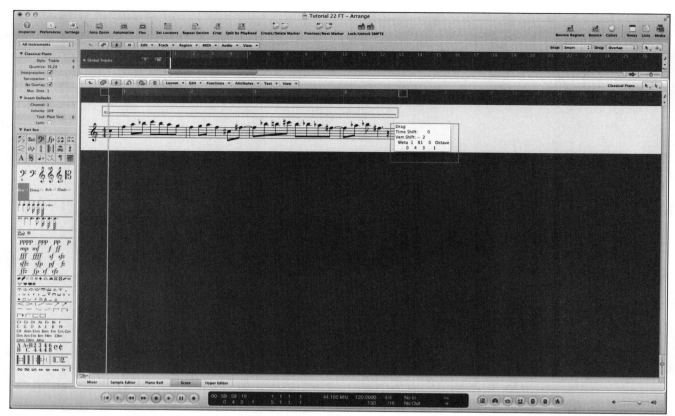

Figure 22.11 Extending the duration of the 8ve up symbol.

Figure 22.12 The violin part with the 8ve up symbol executed properly.

can see my result. Figure 22.17 shows the option for which pages the text should appear on.

3. What if you want a different title? Double-click it to open a dialog box. Click OK for the option to convert it to an editable standard text object, then rename it. In Figure 22.18, I also added an instrument name and a date, aligned left and right, respectively.

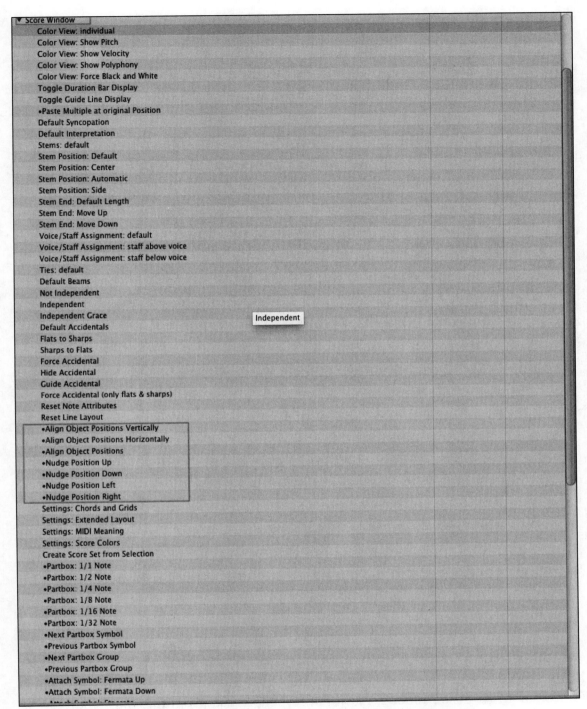

Figure 22.13 Helpful unassigned key commands for positioning symbols.

TEXT	LYRIC	CHORD	REGION
INSTR	SONG	DATE	

Figure 22.14 Additional items available for text insertion.

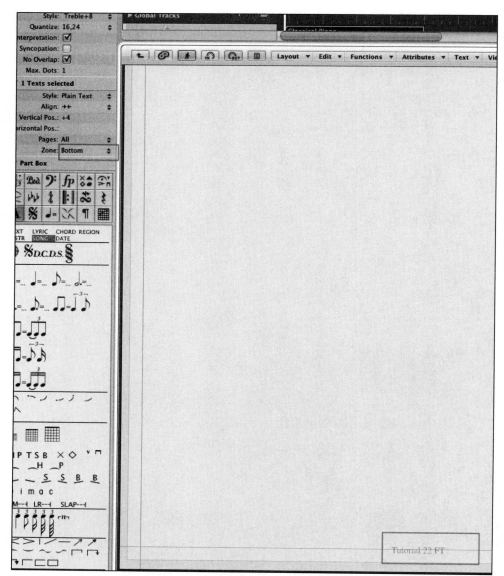

Figure 22.15 The song title inserted at the bottom instead of the desired footer.

Preparing MIDI Files for Transfer to Other Score Apps

You may need help with your score prep on projects with tight deadlines. Believe it or not, some people use Logic Pro for these tasks. Indeed, many more people use programs like Finale or Sibelius. If you will send your work as a standard MIDI file that these apps can use efficiently, you have a little work to do.

Generally, I keep different projects for MIDI sound and for score prep. Therefore, I do not care if doing so changes the sound. I select all the regions to be hard-quantized, and then use the key command for Apply Quantization Destructively. With all the now hard-quantized regions selected, I export them as a standard MIDI file using the .mid suffix.

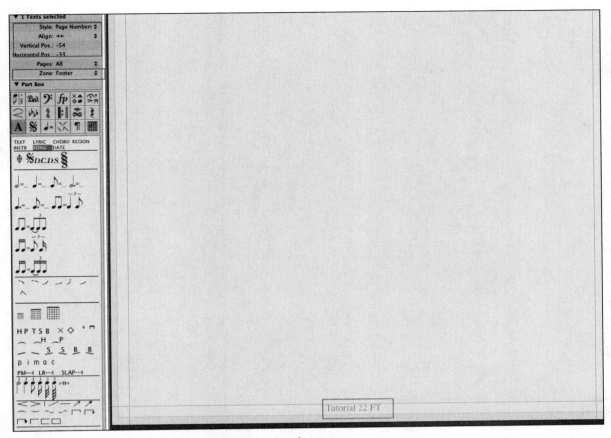

Figure 22.16 Repositioning song title in the footer.

Figure 22.17 Page appearance options.

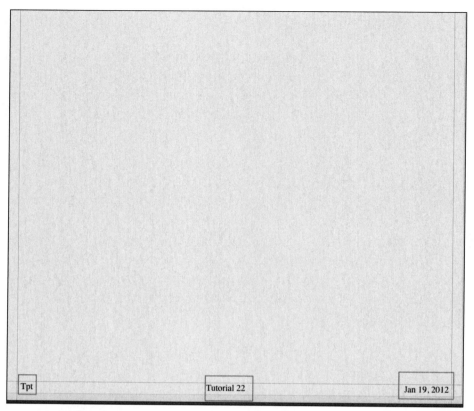

Figure 22.18 The instrument name, renamed song title, and date in the footer.

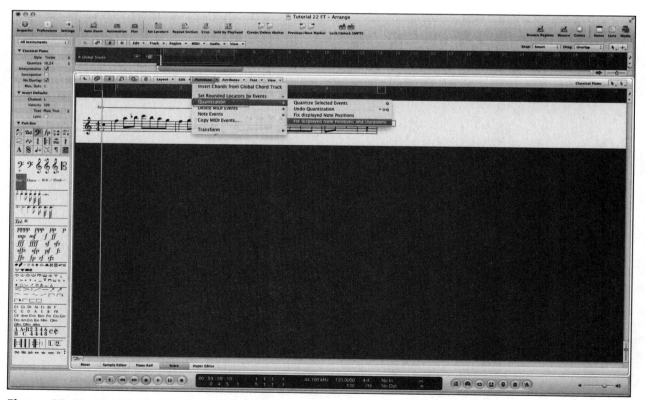

Figure 22.19 Fix Displayed Note Positions and Duration is a Quantization option located under the Functions menu.

However, there is another way to approach this. This tip comes to you courtesy of my intrepid tech editor, composer-orchestrator, and all-around good guy Peter "Ski" Schwartz. See Figure 22.19. If you use the Fix Displayed Note Positions and Durations option on every part, all note durations will be reduced or expanded, as needed, to conform to the exact length of the displayed notes, and their positions will become hard-quantized as well. It effectively "fixes" the lengths and positions of the notes as interpreted by the Score Editor (as opposed to the actual durations and positions of notes).

For example, when playing in an 8th note pizzicato part, the actual notes' played durations might be 16^{ths} or even 32^{nds}. If the part wasn't quantized but still played reasonably in time, setting the display quantization to 8 will create an immediately readable and accurate part; all you would need to do is indicate *pizz*. However, behind the scenes, those notes are still non-quantized and quite short. By using Fix Displayed Note Positions and Durations, the resulting notes in the copyist's MIDI file will be hard-quantized to 8^{ths}, and their duration will be extended to be precisely an 8th note. This can potentially save a composer a considerable amount of money, as the copyist will have to do far less work to make the notes in the MIDI file read correctly in the notation program they are using.

Index

Like the Book?

Let us know on Facebook or Twitter!

facebook.com/courseptr

twitter.com/courseptr

COURSE TECHNOLOGY
CENGAGE Learning
Professional • Technical • Reference

BOOKS FOR THE RECORDING MUSICIAN

Course Technology PTR offers comprehensive resources for musicians and we cover all music and recording topics. Whether you're looking for a book on music production at home or at the studio or a guide to a popular DAW we've got you covered.

The Guitarist's Guide to SONAR
Craig Anderton ■ $29.99

Designed for guitarists of varying levels of experience with music software, this book covers some of the considerations unique to recording guitar with any computer-based system, and then progresses into guitar-specific techniques for Cakewalk SONAR.

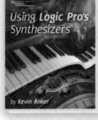

Using Logic Pro's Synthesizers
Kevin Anker ■ $39.99

First, you'll master the simple synthesizers, which will make the essential components of synthesis clear to you. Then, you'll build on that knowledge to learn how to use the more complex synths. In addition, you'll learn about hidden capabilities in the various synths.

Mastering Pro Tools Effects
Getting the Most Out of Pro Tools' Effects Processors
Jeremy Krug ■ $39.99

Offers master-level lessons on using the most essential built-in plug-ins that come with Pro Tools, with detailed descriptions about what each effect is, what each effect does, and how to operate each effect.

Waves Plug-Ins Workshop
Mixing by the Bundle
Barry Wood ■ $29.99

The book on Waves plug-ins! Each chapter introduces the plug-ins in a specific bundle and details how they would be used in a mix.

The Laptop DJ Handbook
Jason Emsley ■ $29.99

Learn to harness all the hardware, software, and musical options available to the modern DJ through helpful explanations, tutorials, and examples.

Pro Tools 101
An Introduction to Pro Tools 10
Avid, Inc. ■ $49.99

This new edition from the definitive authority on Pro Tools covers everything you need to know to complete a Pro Tools project.

New Comprehensive Software Guides from our *Power!* Series

Order now at 1.800.648.7450 or visit courseptr.com

Course Technology PTR products are also available at Guitar Center, Amazon.com, and Barnes and Noble.
All books are also available on Kindle, Nook, iPad, and other digital readers.